Lay Leaders

RESOURCES
FOR THE
CHANGING
PARISH

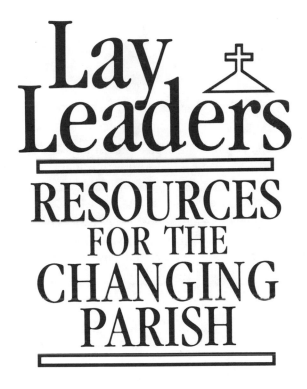

Lay Leaders

RESOURCES FOR THE CHANGING PARISH

William T. Ditewig

AVE MARIA PRESS   Notre Dame, Indiana 46556

Appendix B and portions of Chapter 4 taken from *The Parish Council*, Diocese of Portland, Maine. Used with permission.

Excerpts from *Vatican II: The Conciliar and Post Conciliar Documents*, Austin Flannery, OP, ed. Copyright © 1975 by Costello Publishing Company, Inc., and Reverend Austin Flannery, OP. All rights reserved.

Excerpts from THE NEW JERUSALEM BIBLE, copyright © 1985 by Darton, Longman & Todd, Ltd. and Doubleday & Company, Inc. Reprinted by permission of the publisher.

© 1991 by Ave Maria Press, Notre Dame, IN 46556

International Standard Book Number: 0-87793-443-6

Library of Congress Catalog Card Number: 90-85154

Cover design by Katherine Robinson Coleman.

Printed and bound in the United States of America.

Contents

Introduction ——————————————— 9

CHAPTER 1
Christian Initiation: Immersion Into the Body of Christ—— 11

CHAPTER 2
The People of the Rainbow——————————— 25

CHAPTER 3
Leadership——————————————————— 37

CHAPTER 4
Pastoral Planning—————————————— 49

CHAPTER 5
The Lay Leader and Public Prayer——————— 59

CHAPTER 6
A Pastoral Potpourri————————————— 71

Epilogue———————————————————— 77

Bibliography—————————————————— 79

Appendix A
Canon Law and the Lay Pastor———————— 85

Appendix B
Sample Parish Council Guidelines——————— 91

Acknowledgements

Many people supported this effort, and I am indebted to all of them. In particular, however, I want to thank the following people.

From 1984 to 1987 we were part of two communities of faith: St. Joseph's Parish in Ellsworth, Maine, and the Catholic Chapel community of the Naval Security Group Activity, Winter Harbor, Maine. These communities taught us in a special way the meaning of church. It was an honor to be church with them and we miss them very much.

The graduate faculty and students of the Master of Arts in Pastoral Theology Program at St. Mary-of-the-Woods College, St. Mary-of-the-Woods, Indiana became for us another community of faith and love. The wisdom and experience of these marvelous people put many things in perspective.

I thank Dr. Catherine Dooley, OP, for her kind and most honest reading of the manuscript. The flaws remaining in this work are the result of the author's own inadequacy to express the depth of her insight.

But most especially I acknowledge the loving support of my family, whose patience and love give meaning to everything. Without this community of faith and love, nothing would be possible.

Introduction

This book is a reference tool for lay persons who are or will be in positions of leadership in Catholic parishes. Catholic lay women and men in growing numbers are taking on key roles in decision-making, budgeting, and administering parish affairs. Even more significantly, lay persons are assuming responsibility for providing pastoral care and leadership in these parishes. The U.S. Bishops' Committee on the Liturgy has recently published the results of a survey which indicate that 70 of 167 U.S. dioceses have parishes and missions administered by someone other than a priest; namely, a deacon, religious, or lay person.

But it is too simple to state that the current experience in some parts of the United States is solely the result of Vatican II's strong statements on the nature of the church, on the relationship of the church to the modern world, and the role of the laity in the church. Data from Western Europe[1], Africa, Central and South America, Canada, and selected areas in the United States indicate that the rise of lay leadership in the face of a growing lack of priests is widespread and predates Vatican II.

These data reflect only those lay leaders who may be termed pastors or administrators and do not take into account other persons serving in parish leadership roles. The data point to a significant question: What is the nature of community leadership in the Catholic church? This question has been of concern to the church for a long time. St. Francis Xavier set up Sunday prayer and catechetical meetings in the absence of clergy in sixteenth-century India. Regulations dealing with the same situation in China were published in the seventeenth century.[2] Into our own century priestless communities were of concern to the church. Vatican II briefly alludes to communities without priests in its document on the liturgy by encouraging the use of liturgies of the word on Sundays and holidays, "especially in places where no priest is available" (*Constitution on the Liturgy*, no. 35).

As the church faces greater pastoral and evangelical demands in the modern world with fewer priests, the question many Catholic communities face is one of basic communal identity. Can a parish be "Catholic" without a priest? What is the role and responsibility of lay leadership within any parish, with or without a priest? The answers are being sought by more and more parishes. Many are finding that, with the help of the Spirit, they can form thriving communities using a combined pastoral team of ordained, religious, and non-ordained ministers.

This book is not an attempt to suggest a new ecclesial vision for the future or to espouse a particular view of lay versus ordained ministry. Rather, its purpose is to recognize a real fact of pastoral life in the contemporary church—that for many reasons persons other than priests are being called into pastoral leadership to meet the needs of their local communities and that they need to acquire and develop basic skills to serve effectively. This book seeks to address the need for a handbook for the new pastoral leader.

NOTES

[1] See, for example, the *Pro Mundi Vita: Dossier* #6 of June 1979, which addresses "Priestless Parishes in Western Europe: Present situation and attempted solutions."

[2] J. Frank Henderson, "When Lay People Preside at Sunday Worship," *Worship*, 58 (1984), pp. 108–109.

CHAPTER 1

Christian Initiation: Immersion Into the Body of Christ

INTRODUCTION

The purpose of this chapter is to lay the foundation for what follows by reflecting on the relationship of Christian initiation, the church, and ministry. Only by centering our understanding of ourselves as the people of God united in Christ we can appreciate what ministry ought to be in the church and the world.

What follows may seem so simple and basic that its significance may be lost. Leadership in the church, no matter what form it takes, is grounded in the unity of all believers in Christ. Those who serve are one with those served, and vice versa. What binds all believers together is initiation into the mystery of Christ.

The People of God in History

"We believe in God . . ." begins our creed. We are persons of faith, faith in the almighty and ever-living God who sent the Son to redeem us and the Spirit to enflame us. When Vatican II chose to describe the church as the people of God, it restored to our vocabulary a term rich in history and meaning.

The people of the Old Testament used the expression QA-HAL YAHWEH ("the assembly of God") to describe both their community identity and the head of that community, Yahweh. God called the community into existence and established a covenant, not with individuals, but with the entire assembly. "I will be your God and you shall be my people." This identity as the people of God has sustained the Jewish people throughout its turbulent history. They were the people of God whether they were in captivity in Egypt or Babylonia, worshipping in the Temple of Solomon in Jerusalem, or being slaughtered in the death camps of Nazi Germany.

The people of the New Covenant sought to capture this same sense of community identity in the Christ of Yahweh. The Greek word used to translate QAHAL was EKKLESIA, which we frequently translate as "church," and use in expressions such as "ecclesial" or "ecclesiastic." But the sense of the word is similar to that of the ancient Hebrew text—that this is a people called together by God, who gives the community its life and identity.

The term "assembly" has been restored within liturgical circles to refer to the people of God at prayer. But it is important to note that the public worship of the assembly of God is but one facet, one expression of being "the people of God." "The notion of assembly has foundational significance for anyone attempting to understand the church, the liturgy, or the relationship between the two."[1]

Initiation Into the People of God

When we proclaim our faith, we join with our sisters and brothers to celebrate our union with God and each other. This is our vocation as professed Christians: to give ourselves in service to God and to each other as Christ gave himself in service to God and to us. Baptism is our initiation into the person, mission, and body of Jesus Christ. Although for convenience I am using the word *baptism*, I mean all of the sacraments of initiation: baptism, confirmation, and eucharist. All that a Christian is and does is forever marked by baptism. Baptism into Christ means a rebirth into a new way of life lived in communion with other believers. This assembly of faith, this community called into existence by God, becomes the visible sign of Christ present in the world.

Baptism as Primal Sacrament

The Baltimore Catechism defined a sacrament as "an outward sign instituted by Christ to give grace." The elements contained in that definition are still valuable. A sacrament of the church is a public event that highlights a significant happening in the life of the assembly. Through Christ, the anointed of Yahweh, these public celebrations give life to all members of the community. But all of these celebrations find their roots in the rites of baptism. The sacraments of reconciliation, anointing of the sick, matrimony, and holy orders are all grounded in baptism.

To focus on this primacy of baptism, let's review a bit of history. Our word "sacrament" comes from the Latin word *sacramentum*. The *sacramentum* was the public ritual in which a Roman recruit renounced his former civilian life and assumed his new way of life in military service to the empire and the emperor. There was a two-fold dimension to this ritual. On the one hand, the recruit, as an individual, was affected. His own personal life was forever changed by this action. On the other hand, the community was involved since the recruit was now a "public servant" and responsible to his comrades and his emperor for his actions. The recruit's new status had profound effects on the community as well, for he could no longer live as an individual citizen of Rome. This was more than a change of professions; this was a whole new way of living, a new set of values, a new set of priorities. The *sacramentum* marked a radical turning point in the recruit's life. There was no turning back, and he would never be the same again.

It's easy to see how the young Christian community could use the *sacramentum* to explain the importance of baptism to prospective members. Tertullian, in the second century, was the first to use the term to describe Christian initiation. The Christian *sacramentum* also marked a new beginning, a new allegiance, membership in a new community way of life. St. Augustine would later develop this notion of a radical and permanent change in a person when he wrote of the permanent "seal" of a sacrament. But once again, the effects are both individual and communal. The newly baptized would never be the same again, and the community was augmented and blessed by the new member. The individual being baptized would not live out this new life of faith in a vacuum; rather, faith would find its articulation in and through and with other people.

This two-fold dimension of baptism is stressed in the newly restored Rite of Christian Initiation For Adults (RCIA). Throughout the RCIA process, the community of the baptized participates in the journey of its newest members. Initiation is not just something done to or for the catechumens, it is something shared with them. When we celebrate the sacraments of initiation at the Easter Vigil, we celebrate and renew our own initiation along with the catechumens. They are changed forever. So are we. The moment is one of awesome and wonderful dimension, as the entire people of God celebrates its oneness in God, its total and radical rebirth in Christ.

Do we have other examples in human experience of the intensity of such an event? Consider the following non-Christian example, drawn from the novel *Shogun* by James Clavell.

In this story, a seventeenth-century English ship's pilot, John Blackthorne, is shipwrecked in Japan and caught up in a culture completely mysterious to him. To survive, the pilot must assimilate these new cultural values. At one point, a warlord demands that he learn Japanese as quickly as possible or else all of the inhabitants of the pilot's village will be executed. To show his abhorrence of the order, the pilot, called *anjin-san* by the Japanese, threatens to take his own life in the Japanese manner rather than to live with the shame of being responsible for the deaths of innocent victims. Since the authorities are convinced that as a Christian the pilot will never take his own life, they call his bluff. The pilot prepares to carry out his threat. As he faces death, he realizes with great clarity that he is not afraid of death and that what he is about to do is the right thing. As he thrusts the knife toward his abdomen, he is restrained and prevented from injuring himself.

The significance of this episode for us lies in its aftermath. Faced with the inevitability and awesomeness of his own death, the pilot achieves an inner clarity he had not known before. He reaches a new level of being, what we have called above a radical new beginning to his life. Consider the words of the novelist:

> Blackthorne came back from death slowly. He stared at them and the knife from an immense distance, without

understanding. Then the torrent of his life rushed back but he could not grasp its significance, believing himself dead and not alive. . . . I'm alive, he told himself in wonder. I'm alive and that's real rain outside and the wind's real and from the north. There's a real brazier with real coals and if I pick up the cup it will have real liquid in it and it will have taste. I'm not dead, I'm alive![2]

From that moment on, Blackthorne's life is changed forever. His relationships with others and even his relationship with himself have been altered permanently. His experience has profound impact on those who observe him and those with whom he lives.

Consider this example from our own history. Dallas. November 22, 1963. The Texas Book Depository. Motorcade. For people old enough to remember, these few words call to mind an event indelibly scrawled across the pages of our personal and communal lives: President John F. Kennedy had been murdered. The nation was traumatized. Newscasters wept on the air. Young people lost innocence. Older people lost hope. Regardless of political party, religion, or social status, everyone was affected. This was one of those events that transfix an individual person within a particular moment in history. Everyone who experienced it can recount vividly what he or she was doing upon hearing the news. The death of Franklin Delano Roosevelt, the attack on Pearl Harbor, and the stock market crash of 1929 are other examples.

Similar events happen within our personal lives as well: the birth of a child, the loss of a parent or spouse, a wedding or ordination—all mark a turning point from which there is no return. Our lives are forever changed for good or ill.

Consider now these words of St. Paul:

You cannot have forgotten that all of us, when we were baptized into Christ Jesus, were baptized into his death. So by our baptism into his death we were buried with him, so that as Christ was raised from the dead by the Father's glorious power, we too should begin living a new life. If we have been joined to him by dying a death like his, so we shall be by a resurrection like his (Rom 6:3–5).

In the New Covenant, the human experience of living life after facing death takes on even more significance when we realize that we are talking about so much more than merely physical existence. In baptism, our entire beings are transformed "through Christ, with Christ, and in Christ." We are faced, not just with a different human culture, but with a truly new way of existence. What a magnificent and awesome moment baptism is!

The challenge to all of us is to rediscover the awesomeness and wonder of this experience, and to begin to appreciate the stupendous implications it has on the way we live our lives. It was for this reason that one of the very first things Vatican II directed was that the period of pre-baptismal preparation known as the catechumenate be restored. Likewise, it was for this reason that the U.S. bishops have mandated this restored catechumenate, now known as the RCIA, for all parishes in the United States. The message of our renewed understanding of baptism is clear: Baptism marks the beginning of a new existence for the newly baptized as the neophyte joins with the rest of the people of God in its journey of faith.

Baptism and the People of God: Vatican II

But once the "turning point" of baptism has been reached, what then? How do we live out this new life within the framework of the people of God? Just who is this community of faith? For some answers, we'll turn to the documents of Vatican II and the revised *Code of Canon Law*. The revised *Code* has been called "the seventeenth document of Vatican II," both because the revision itself was mandated by the Council and because it codifies much of the theology of the council.

In the sixteenth century, St. Robert Bellarmine articulated a definition of the church that was accepted and taught into our own century.

What is the Church?
The Church is the congregation of all baptized persons united in the same true faith, the same sacrifice, and the same sacraments, under the authority of the Sovereign Pontiff and the bishops in communion with him.

Although the church has continued to develop its sense of identity in different terms, notice that our understanding always starts with the notion of the assembly of the baptized. Over the years we have sometimes focused more on the institutional or structural elements of the church, but today we see a return to the very ground and sign of our unity: baptism.

Much of the impetus behind this renewed appreciation of the centrality of baptism and its impact on our communal life can be traced to Vatican II and its *Dogmatic Constitution on the Church* (*Lumen Gentium*). In this now-classic document, the church looks inward upon itself and seeks to articulate a new vision of the very nature and mission of the church.

The first chapter is devoted to calling forth a biblical understanding of the nature of the church. The church is the assembly of believers in Christ. "The origin and growth of the church are symbolized by the blood and water which flowed from the open side of the crucified Jesus" (*Constitution on the Church*, no. 3). The community of faith is thus joined to the sacrifice of Jesus, as expressed in a special way in our eucharistic celebration. The Holy Spirit gives gifts to the community "and in this way directs her; and he adorns her with his fruits" (*Constitution on the Church*, no. 4). Through the Spirit the church is constantly renewed. All who believe in Christ are joined by baptism into this community of faith. While there is a hierarchical organization to this community, "the society structured with hierarchical organs and the mystical body of Christ . . . are not to be thought of as two realities. On the contrary, they form one complex reality which comes together from a human and a divine element" (*Constitution on the Church*, no. 8). It is important to remember that the Greek word *laos*, from which we get our word *laity*, includes all members of the faith community. *Laos* includes bishops, priests, and deacons as well as the non-ordained. Baptism is the primal sacrament by which all become members of *laos*, the people of God.

The second chapter echoes the words of Peter, that all the baptized are established as "a chosen race, a royal priesthood, a holy nation . . . who in times past were not a people, but now are the people of God" (*Constitution on the Church*, no. 9, quoting 1 Pet 2:9–10). This theme is developed throughout the chapter, culminating in the vital understanding that through baptism we are called to share in the priesthood of Christ. To live out the covenant is not the role of a priestly caste; rather, all believers are baptized into the covenant. The Council develops the specific functions of the clergy and laity, but both are united to form the one people of God. Together we share the responsibility to nurture and challenge the communities in which we live.

Another area in which the *Constitution on the Church* speaks to our particular subject is in its discussion of the local church. While this section is focused primarily on the diocesan church, we can, I think, gain valuable insight into the nature of the parish church as well:

> [The] Church of Christ is really present in all legitimately organized local groups of the faithful, which, insofar as they are united to their pastors, are also quite appropriately called Churches in the New Testament. For these are in fact, in their own localities, the new people called by God, in the power of the Holy Spirit and as the result of full conviction. . . . In these communities, though they may often be small and poor, or existing in the diaspora, Christ is present through whose power and influence the One, Holy, Catholic and Apostolic Church is constituted (*Constitution on the Church*, no. 26).

The point here is that the local church is not merely a pale reflection of the universal church. It is a full expression of the church of Christ. Leonard Doohan observes that John Paul II "refers to these small cells of ecclesial life as the foundation of the church and sees them as constituting the church in its essential dimension."[3] Before Vatican II, most people thought of the Catholic church only as the large, international organization it is. Now we see a shift of focus, not denying the universality of the church, but rather seeing the church as a mosaic, a "cloak of many colors," made up of local assemblies of the faithful who are, by virtue of the baptism they share in common, the church.

Baptism and the People of God: The Code of Canon Law

Before we conclude this chapter, it would be useful to review the position of the 1983 *Code of Canon Law*. This may seem a bit unusual, but the *Code* is very important to this discussion. Although the *Code* appeared in 1983, its revision was directed by Vatican II. Since the earlier documents of the Council helped redefine our understanding of church, we may also assume that the specific guidelines and procedures given in the revised *Code* would be consistent and in harmony with the Council. In other words, where the earlier documents focused a bit more on the general theological principles involved in redefining church, the *Code* offers specific practical applications of that theory.

In addition, the *Code* gives lay pastoral leaders a good outline of where and how lay ministry fits into the life of the church. As we shall see, it addresses many things, from the nature of the church itself, to specific procedures to be followed in various pastoral situations.

Mary Moisson Chandler has done a very good introduction to this area in her book *The Pastoral Associate and the Lay Pastor*. She offers some very important things to keep in mind as we consider the revised *Code*:

- The Church is a community of persons, not a hierarchically dominated state.
- This community is fundamentally equal through baptism. No longer is the Church to be seen as a two-tiered society [clergy-laity].
- Subsidiarity is a basic working principle. This means that the responsibility of governing and decision-making is not to be found at the highest level, but at the most appropriate level. Bishops, dioceses, and parishes are to have more of an impact on participating in governing rather than just being governed from above.
- The official ministry of the Church is not to be one of status and privilege, but one of service.[4]

Chandler summarizes the spirit of the revised Code very well by speaking of the baptized person's call to mission, call to gifts, and call to ministry. Our call to mission is to proclaim the kingdom of God through lives of holiness and evangelization. Our call to gifts addresses the charisms we receive to carry out our mission. Through these gifts we are enabled and obliged to be informed and to live out the mission we share as church. Lastly, our call to ministry demands that we participate to the extent God's gifts enable us in works of liturgy, charity, and service. Notice that these are calls to all baptized Christians, not just to ordained ministers.

Let's review specific canons to see just how lay pastoral leaders participate in the official ministry of the church. This review should be useful for your entire community so that everyone can realize that the universal church fully recognizes the role of the lay leader. The canons are: 230, 517, 519, 528, 529, 759, 766, 767, 773, 776, 861, 911, 943, 1112, 1248, 1282 and 1289. The text of these canons may be found in appendix A.

Canon 230 addresses the liturgical functions normally associated with the installed ministries of lector and acolyte. Germane to our discussion is the fact that this canon allows persons who are not installed in these ministries to perform their functions. Canons 517 and 519 discuss the role of the pastor, and also allows the appointment of persons other than priests to serve in a pastoral capacity as long as a priest is assigned as supervisor. Canons 528 and 529 continue the discussion of the role of pastor. They are important to our discussion, however, since many lay pastoral leaders carry out these functions.

Canons 759, 766, 767 and 1248 (§2) pertain to the participation of lay persons in the liturgy of the word, particularly with regard to preaching. While preaching homilies during Mass is reserved to priests and deacons by canon 767, other forms of preaching are permissible, and homilies by lay persons at services other than Mass (such as a liturgy of the word coupled with the Rite of Communion Outside Mass) are permissible.

Canons 861, 911, 943, and 1112 all refer to lay persons performing other sacramental functions. Canon 861 permits a catechist "or other person deputed for this function" to confer baptism. Canon 911 pertains to the bringing of *viaticum* to the sick, canon 943 addresses the exposition and reposition of the eucharist by lay persons (without benediction, which is reserved to a priest or deacon), and canon 1112 permits (with the permission of the Holy See) lay persons to assist at marriages "where priests or deacons are lacking."

SUMMARY

In summary, then, baptism is the key to everything which follows, both in our lives and in this book. The essence of what we're about in service to each other is contained in our baptisms.

1. Baptism is the primal sacrament upon which all others are based.

2. The effects of baptism are relational: they pertain to the way we relate to God and to each other.

3. Baptism is the very core of the way we are church together, both as worldwide church and as local church.

James Dunning offers this important observation:

> For the believer, only God can build real community. Our faith is that people do not live this astonishing life of self-giving love, made flesh especially in Jesus, unless God gives us such power. Our faith also is that our ministries of building community are not self-initiated. They are ultimately a sharing of gifts which are initiated and brought to birth in us by God.[5]

QUESTIONS FOR REFLECTION

How has baptism affected your life? Has it made a difference in the person you are? How?

Are effects of baptism evident in your local parish? How do the baptized members of the community relate to the unbaptized (such as catechumens) in their midst?

How are baptisms handled in your parish? Are they celebrations of the entire community? Or are they private, single-family affairs?

Who works with persons or families seeking baptism? Pastor only? Deacon? Committee? Combination of the above? How does this affect the way baptism is perceived by your parish?

Baptism is referred to above as "the primal sacrament." What does this mean to you?

FOR FURTHER READING

History can teach us many things and help us put our own experiences in perspective. There are any number of good histories of the church; two good popular histories are Father William Bausch's *Pilgrim Church* and Father Thomas Bokenkotter's *Concise History of the Catholic Church*. If you'd like a very good concise history of the parish, see chapter one of Father Thomas Sweetser, SJ and Carol Wisniewski's book, *Leadership in the Successful Parish*. They provide an informative overview of "The History of the Parish" and "The Parish Today."

For more information on baptism, see Father Joseph Martos, *Doors to the Sacred*, or Father Bausch's *New Look at the Sacraments*. Not only will these works give a good understanding of the sacrament of baptism, they also show the relationship of the other sacraments to baptism. *The New Dictionary of Theology*, edited by Joseph Komonchak, Mary Collins, and Dermot Lane, contains excellent articles on baptism, the assembly, and related topics.

Full bibliographic details on these works may be found at the end of the book. These suggestions are offered merely to get you started. There are many fine works available on the sacraments; I've found these to be particularly readable and adaptable to a variety of pastoral situations.

NOTES

[1] Margaret Mary Kelleher, OSU, *"Assembly"* in *The New Dictionary of Theology*, Joseph A. Komonchak, Mary Collins, Dermot A. Lane, eds., (Wilmington, DE: Michael Glazier, Inc., 1987), p. 67.

[2] James Clavell, *Shogun: A Novel of Japan*, (New York: Atheneum, 1975), pp. 464–465.

[3] Leonard Doohan, *Laity's Mission in the Local Church* (San Francisco, CA: Harper & Row, 1986), p. 27.

[4] Mary Moisson Chandler, *The Pastoral Associate and the Lay Pastor*, (Collegeville, MN: The Liturgical Press, 1983), p. 25.

[5] Dunning, James, *Ministries: Sharing God's Gifts* (Winona, MN: St. Mary's Press, 1985), p. 62.

CHAPTER 2

The People
of the Rainbow

INTRODUCTION

"I now set my bow in the clouds and it will be the sign of
the covenant between me and the earth . . . . When the
bow is in the clouds I shall see it and call to mind the
eternal covenant between God and every living crea-
ture on earth, that is, all living things." "That," God
told Noah, "is the sign of the covenant I have established between myself and all living things on earth"
(Gn 9:13, 16–17).

The rainbow is an ancient sign of the covenant to which we
are called. It is a sign that our community of faith is the
joining of a loving God with a loving people. In this chapter
our focus will be on the unique characteristics of the Christian community of faith, keeping in mind that the church is
more than group dynamics and social interaction. The church
is a mystery and a sacrament which defies comprehensive human definition. The church is the making present in human
experience the loving action of God through the person of Jesus
Christ. The church is God and people together, what theolo-
gian Edward Schillebeeckx calls "the sacrament of the human
encounter with God."

Evelyn and James Whitehead describe the community of
faith in this way:

In the end, the formation of the community of faith
remains the work of the Spirit. A well-structured group
that is clear in its goals, open in its communication, and
committed to its religious values may still flounder. Life
remains that ambiguous; faith, that much a mystery. But
the person who is aware of the social dynamics of group

25

life and sensitive to the purpose and particular history of this group can contribute importantly to the possibility of community. And the possibility of community is the hope in which we stand, awaiting the gracious visitation of our God.[1]

This chapter will examine the church as characterized by the ancient "marks" of the church. Namely, that it is one, holy, catholic, and apostolic. After a brief reflection on the development of these marks in the Christian tradition, we will explore each of them in greater depth.

The Marks of the Church

The whole group of believers was united, heart and soul; no one claimed private ownership of any possessions, as everything they owned was held in common. The apostles continued to testify to the resurrection of the Lord Jesus with great power, and they were all accorded great respect. None of their members was ever in want, as all those who owned land or houses would sell them, and bring the money from the sale of them, to present it to the apostles; it was then distributed to any who might be in need (Acts 4:32–25).

Does this sound like a description of your parish? Probably not. Consider some of the elements Luke uses: one heart, one mind; communal ownership of property; powerful preaching and Christian witness; no needy or homeless; everything used to meet the needs of those with nothing. What are the signs that would proclaim to the world today the unique nature of the people of God?

Since the fourth century, the Christian church has proclaimed its belief in "one holy catholic and apostolic church" (the Nicene Creed). Over the years, these marks (or "signs" or "notes") of the church have been used in prayer, catechesis, and apologetics. While these terms were a treasured part of our Christian heritage long before the Reformation, since the Reformation and up until the time of Vatican II, these marks of the church were used most frequently to illustrate the authenticity

of the Roman Catholic church. Consider, for example, this dialogue from the Baltimore Catechism:

> *How do we know that the Catholic Church is the one true*
> *Church established by Christ?*
> We know that the Catholic Church is the one true
> Church established by Christ because it alone has the
> marks of the true church. . . [which] are four: It is one,
> holy, catholic or universal, and apostolic.

The point here is that these four marks of the church were
not originally intended to serve as a means of distinguishing
authentic from unauthentic churches. Rather, they were distinguishing attributes of the entire Christian church as compared
to the non-Christian world. Vatican II restored these marks to
their proper focus when it proclaimed:

> This is the sole Church of Christ which in the Creed we
> profess to be one, holy, catholic and apostolic. . . . This
> Church, constituted and organized as a society in the
> present world, subsists in the Catholic Church. . . .
> Nevertheless, many elements of sanctification and of
> truth are found outside its visible confines. Since these
> are gifts belonging to the church of Christ, they are
> forces impelling toward Catholic unity (*Constitution on*
> *the Church*, no. 8).

The church of Christ exists in its fullness in the Catholic church,
but is not limited to it. There is another element added by the
Council. The marks of the church are not just static attributes,
but "forces impelling toward Catholic unity." Bernard Marthaler,
in his book *The Creed*, tells us that the marks of the church are
"not only endowments given to the church by the holy Spirit but
also tasks that challenge the church at every level. . . ."[2] The
U.S. bishops, in *Sharing the Light of Faith: National Catechetical*
Directory for Catholics of the United States, call the marks "gifts
bestowed upon the church by the Lord—but gifts which the
church must also strive to realize ever more fully in its life."[3]

These, then, are the marks of the church. As we examine each of them, remember that these marks, these challenges,

these gifts, have been given to the entire church, in its universal and its local manifestations. Our purpose here is to consider how they are held in our particular local church.

The Church Is One

We, the people of God, are one in Jesus Christ, "of one heart and of one mind." Jesus' great prayer for the unity of the church concludes the Last Supper, "May they all be one, just as, Father, you are in me and I am in you" (Jn 17:21). The mark of unity is of central importance, for, according to Macquarrie, "in its fullest sense, the unity of the church implies its holiness, catholicity, and apostolicity."[4]

But what does it mean to be one? As human persons we take pride in our uniqueness and individuality. What is the relationship between an individual and a community? How do we as church deal with the individual persons who make up our community? How do we find unity in diversity? The church has used many images over the years to describe this phenomenon. We began this chapter using the rainbow as a sign of God's covenant. The rainbow is one glorious experience made from different colors. But without the colors, the rainbow would cease to be. Consider Paul's image of the body of Christ, with Christ as head and the members of the church as the rest of the body. Still another New Testament image, that of the vine and the branches, comes to mind. Scripture never lets us forget that people are taken into the covenant community as unique individuals who now center themselves around Christ.

The plain fact is this: unity does not mean uniformity. Bernard Marthaler cites Yves Congar's *Diversity and Communion*, saying, "Nothing in the New Testament suggests that uniformity—the denial of diversity—is an ideal, and the history of the church is evidence that it has never been a reality."[5] The implications of this fact on our local parishes are the same as for the universal church. We may all be one in our faith in Jesus Christ as Lord, but disagree on just about everything else. How do we as church deal with those who disagree with us? Are we open to the diversity of our communities, the colors of our rainbow, or do we try to coerce uniformity?

A fine line must be drawn here. The church is called to oneness in faith, hope, and love, but we are not called to be mindless robots, checking our unique, God-given personalities at the door. On the contrary, we are called to be as totally human as we can be, unique creations of the one God. The community has the right to expect a unity of faith, but it cannot stifle the creativity and imagination of its members.

The world watches when the universal church deals with dissent. Hans Kung and George Stallings appeared on *The Phil Donohue Show*. Charles Curran debated his positions with Archbishop James Hickey on television as well as in the courts. As important as these events have been, how do we deal with dissent in our own parish? How do values of unity, uniformity, and diversity interact?

Evelyn Eaton Whitehead and James D. Whitehead, in *Community of Faith: Models and Strategies for Developing Christian Community*, have examined the continuing formation of the Christian faith community, providing valuable insight into the forces at work in the Christian community. The Whiteheads talk about the three basic views of diversity that people hold: diversity as scandal, diversity as relativism, and diversity as a sign of richness.

Diversity as Scandal. In this view, any notion of diversity is taken as something bad which needs to be eliminated. The credal statement of "one catholic church" is understood to mean that there can be one and only one way to believe and act. Frequently, the person who holds this view of diversity will become almost violent over the subject of change or any perceived threat to the orthodoxy of the community. The danger with this view is that it is very defensive in nature: you find what is to be preserved and build a wall around it to protect it. But when walls are built to keep danger out, people frequently find themselves imprisoned.

Diversity as Relativism. If you get into a lively debate with a person who holds the "diversity-as-scandal" view, you may find yourself accused of relativism: everything and anything is acceptable. While this perspective may seem to avoid conflict (How can anyone be unhappy if any view is acceptable?), it actually devalues the issue at hand and stifles the healthy dialogue which should take place in a living, adult community. Instead you wind up with a group of individuals with no convictions.

The danger here is that instead of building a community of faith, you have an association of individuals, each with a private set of values and beliefs.

Diversity as a Sign of Richness.   In this view, the key element is balance. It steers between the Scylla and Charibdis of the other two positions. This view accepts the fact that, in the final analysis, no human person knows the mind of God. Our shared human experiences of God in our lives become the bits and pieces of the divine mosaic. Somewhere between the rocks of rigid authoritarianism and the shoals of relativism lies the true course for the ship of faith.

Actually the best model of unity-in-diversity for the church is the trinity itself: three persons in one God. Consider again the prayer of Jesus, "That all may be one, as you, Father are in me, and I in you." Without the loss of individual personhood, the members of the trinity are so intimately bound together that no one can adequately explain the mystery. John Macquarrie describes the Holy Spirit as "unitive Being," whose role is "the drawing out of the potentialities of creation at all levels."[6] In fact, according to Marthaler, "the Western church has traditionally ascribed to the holy Spirit a unitive function within the Trinity. . . . The mission of the holy Spirit in the world is seen as uniting believers to one another and to God in the Body of Christ."[7] In short, the unity of the church is both an attribute and a challenge: We are one but we are called to continuing efforts at greater unity.

The challenge to pastoral leaders that this mark proclaims centers on the theme of reconciliation through the action of the Spirit. One of the greatest scandals of the ages is the division and cruelty of Christian against Christian, and Christian against non-Christian. The leaders of the Christian community are charged to inspire and enable all persons to focus on the things that unite rather than those that divide. Only through the action of the Spirit in the life of the community can ways be found to surrender egocentric individualism in favor of the common good. On the night before he died, Jesus could have defended himself before Pilate and been released to continue his life and ministry. He even pleaded with his Father to take the cup of suffering away from him. Instead, he became vulnerable unto death for the salvation of the world. His actions challenge us to do no less than to spend ourselves totally for the good of the kingdom. We are not a community of faith for ourselves, but for each other and for God.

The Church Is Holy

In *Sharing the Light of Faith*, the U.S. bishops tell us:

Its union with Christ gives the church a holiness which can never fail and empowers it to foster holiness it its members. This holiness, engendered by the Spirit, is expressed in the lives of Christians who strive to grow in charity and to help others do the same (no. 72, reference to 1 Cor 3:16ff).

Historically speaking, "holy" was the first mark attributed to the church. Marthaler cites second- and third-century sources that indicate that "holy" was becoming a "stock epithet" to describe the church.[8] But, as with all the marks of the church, there is a two-fold dimension: We are a holy people called to greater holiness.

Why and how are we holy? We know ourselves to be sinful and in a state of continuing conversion to the Lord. How can we be so presumptuous as to call ourselves a holy people? Our bishops give us the answer: "This holiness [is] engendered by the Spirit." We are the holy people of God because God is present in our midst. The mystery which is church is not holy because of the individual holiness of its human members, but because of the presence of the all-holy God.

The holy ones of the church—the saints—show us the path from sin to sanctity illuminated by the Spirit to whom we are all called. We are part of the communion of saints, a community of holy ones called to share in the holiness of God. This link with the divine is grace, and, according to "the visible embodiment of the church's holiness is its sacramental life."[9] Through the sacraments, which Joseph Martos aptly calls "the doors to the sacred," we share in the presence of God in our midst. As one people, we are made holy in the sight of God.

The pastoral challenge is to keep the continuing call to sanctity forever present in the community. We are pilgrims in a pilgrim church, following the path to union with God. Since God is with us on the journey, we are already holy; since the journey continues, we are challenged to greater holiness. As leaders in the community, we are called to enhance its sacramental life, not just through the seven sacraments of the church, but through all persons, events, and things that serve as doors to the sacred.

The Church Is Catholic

Sharing the Light of Faith goes on to describe how the church is catholic: "The catholicity or universality of the church rests on the fact that the gospel message is capable of being integrated with all cultures. It corresponds to all that is authentically human" (no. 72). Notice how this mark rests on the concept of unity already discussed: The one church potentially embraces all of humanity. The term *catholic* understood in this universal sense was in use long before it became a statement of orthodoxy. In fact, it is rather ironic that this term should have developed a sectarian connotation since it denotes exactly the opposite!

Macquarrie offers a view which might explain how this phenomenon took place.

> "Catholicity" also means authenticity, that is to say, authenticity of belief and practice in the Church. This second meaning is related to the first, for it has in view the consensus of the Church. The authentic faith is to be learned by considering the universal faith. So from New Testament times onward, we find that when some weighty matter is to be decided, this is done by summoning a council and ascertaining the consensus of the Church.[10]

How is the catholicity of the church experienced in our time? Probably the most obvious example for many of us would be the Second Vatican Council. As Macquarrie points out, councils of the church have been a method used since New Testament times to resolve serious issues. In the case of Vatican II, the issue was to proclaim its identity and mission within the context of the modern world.

The key element of catholicity is its openness to all persons. Macquarrie, for example, ties the concept of catholicity to creation itself. God's covenant is with all humankind, and the church is called to proclaim that good news throughout the world: Go and baptize all nations. All of creation itself is to be brought into the kingdom. For the local church this means being inclusive, not exclusive. Indeed the only way for the universal church to be truly catholic is for the local manifestations of that church to stand with arms opened wide in welcome.

Jesus excluded no one from discipleship; in fact, he went out of his way to include even those whom common wisdom would have excluded. Jesus embraced lepers (Do we embrace the victims of AIDS in our midst?); Jesus welcomed sinners (Do we forgive the sins of others, or hold a grudge?); Jesus took in the socially unacceptable (How do we welcome those who don't fit our idea of what a Christian should be like?). If modern-day lepers, sinners, or the socially unacceptable were on the outside of your parish looking in, how would they feel? Welcomed? Excited about the warmth and joy those in the parish obviously feel? Or would they feel intimidated and rejected? Is your parish an open group or a closed one?

Not everyone wants to join the church; that's a decision a person makes individually or in prayer with God. But all should feel that the church would welcome them, and that their presence in the community would make a difference.

The Church Is Apostolic

This sign has both a historical and dynamic significance. The historical significance is that the church is one with Christ and the original witnesses to Christ—the apostles. The church has remained faithful to the person and mission of Christ throughout the centuries. The dynamic significance derives from the meaning of the word "apostle"—one who is sent. We are an apostolic church because we—like the apostles—are sent to continue the work of Jesus in the world today.

If the mark of catholicity refers to our stance vis-a-vis the world, the mark of apostolicity refers to the movement of the open community into the world. To be open to others is not enough for the Christian community. We are called to follow in the footsteps of the apostles who were sent to proclaim the good news—to be missionaries wherever we find ourselves. Marthaler says, "It must be stressed that apostolic witness is always directed forward in time."[11] We are rooted in the past but called to a future when the kingdom will be established in its fullness.

How apostolic is your parish? Is there a sense of mission outside of itself? If we tend to be a closed group, how can we call ourselves catholic; if we are totally self-contained, how can we call ourselves apostolic? The challenge to pastoral leadership is to allow the Spirit to so fill the community that it overflows into the wider world as well.

SUMMARY

Almost from the beginning of the Christian church, it has been known as one, holy, catholic, and apostolic. Two things should be remembered about these marks of the church. First, they are not only attributes the church already possesses (therefore assuring some measure of authenticity), they are also tasks or challenges the church is called to perpetuate. Secondly, we usually think of these marks only in relation to the universal church. While they most definitely exist there, we must also remember that these are also the marks our parish also shares. St. John's Parish in Peoria, Illinois is and must be one, holy, catholic, and apostolic, just as Sacred Heart Parish in Bowie, Maryland and St. Joseph Parish in Ellsworth, Maine. We, as the people of God in a given location and time, are called to reflect these marks in all we are and all we do.

QUESTIONS FOR REFLECTION

Read the description of the early Christian community again (Acts 4:32–25). What does your parish look like? If you were Luke, what words would you use to describe your community? Try writing down your description, using the following questions as a guide:

What does it mean for a "community of believers" to be of "one heart and one mind"?
- heart (feelings?)
- mind (intellect? way of seeing things?)
- Can any group feel and perceive things "as one"?
- Is diversity seen as a source of dissension or as a powerful resource within the parish?

What do we claim as "our own"?
- Does all we have exist for the common good?
- How do we share time, treasure, and talent?
- What's mine, ours, and the church's?

What does it mean to bear witness powerfully to the resurrection of the Lord Jesus?
- Who are our apostles today?
- In other words, "Whose job is it?"
- How do we "bear witness":
  - through preaching?
  - by teaching?
  - in living?
- Witness equals martyr
  - Am I ready to go that far?
  - Is our parish ready to go that far?
  - What does the resurrection mean to me?
  - How do we "respect" today's apostles?

What is the place of . . .
- obedience?
- reverence?
- love and friendship?
- dialogue?

Who are the needy here and now?
- the homeless, AIDS victims, the infirm?

- abandoned, abused children?
- those without hope?
What do we do about those in need?
- Have we "sold our houses"?
- Do we give up everything to help others?
- Or do we have our own agenda?

FOR FURTHER READING

In addition to the works already cited within this chapter, I would recommend Bausch's *The Christian Parish*, Dunning's *Ministries: Sharing God's Gifts*, and Burke and Hemrick's *Building the Local Church: Shared Responsibility in Diocesan Pastoral Councils*. Full bibliographic details are provided at the end of the book.

NOTES

[1] Evelyn E. Whitehead and James D. Whitehead, *Community of Faith: Models and Strategies for Developing Christian Communities* (Minneapolis, MN: Winston Seabury Press, 1982), p. 60.

[2] Bernard L. Marthaler, *The Creed* (Mystic, CT: Twenty-Third Publications, 1987), pp. 306–307.

[3] *Sharing the Light of Faith: National Catechetical Directory for Catholics of the United States* (Washington, DC: United States Catholic Conference, 1979), no. 72.

[4] John Macquarrie, *Principles of Christian Theology*, second edition (New York: Charles Scribner's Sons, 1977), p. 402.

[5] Marthaler, *The Creed*, p. 308.

[6] Macquarrie, *Principles of Christian Theology*, pp. 328–329.

[7] Marthaler, *The Creed*, p. 308.

[8] Marthaler, *The Creed*, p. 312.

[9] Macquarrie, *Principles of Christian Theology*, p. 406.

[10] Macquarrie, *Principles of Christian Theology*, p. 407.

[11] Marthaler, *The Creed*, p. 317.

CHAPTER 3

Leadership

INTRODUCTION

Baptized into Christ, we can say with St. Paul, "I have been crucified with Christ and yet I am alive; yet it is no longer I, but Christ living in me" (Gal 2:19–20). We turn to Christ to find what he himself has to say about leadership in a Christian community. How did Christ, who now lives in us, lead? How do we, who are Christ in the world, lead?

> But Jesus called them to him and said, "You know that among the gentiles the rulers lord it over them, and great men make their authority felt. Among you this is not to happen. No; anyone who wants to become great among you must be your servant, and anyone who wants to be first among you must be your slave, just as the Son of man came not to be served but to serve, and to give his life as a ransom for many" (Mt 20:25–28).

> (T)he greatest among you must behave as if he were the youngest, the leader as if he were the one who serves. For who is the greater: the one at table or the one who serves? The one at table, surely! Yet here am I among you as one who serves! (Lk 22:26–27).

Building on this theme of servant-leadership learned from the master, St. Peter also teaches us about leadership in Christ:

> Each one of you has received a special grace, so, like good stewards responsible for all these varied graces of God, put it at the service of others. If anyone is a speaker, let it be as the words of God, if anyone serves, let it be as in strength granted by God; so that in everything God may receive the glory, through Jesus Christ, since to him alone belong all glory and power for ever and ever. Amen (1 Pet 4:10–11).

> I urge the elders among you, as a fellow-elder myself and
> a witness to the sufferings of Christ, and as one who is
> to have a share in the glory that is to be revealed: give
> a shepherd's care to the flock of God that is entrusted
> to you: watch over it, not simply as a duty but gladly, as
> God wants; not for sordid money, but because you are
> eager to do it. Do not lord it over the group which is in
> your charge, but be an example for the flock. When the
> chief shepherd appears, you will be given the unfading
> crown of glory (1 Pet 5:1–4).

In a certain sense, some Christians think of leadership as
something for which they are not qualified. Parents worry that
they don't know enough to teach their children about faith.
Some people tend to avoid taking responsibility for a parish
project for the same reason. They may even feel unworthy.
Others may feel leadership is un-Christian. For example, on the
opening day of a formation program for permanent deacons, the
new candidates were told that they were going to be (and in
fact, already were) leaders in the church. One man disagreed
rather heatedly, saying that he was becoming a deacon to be
a servant, not a leader. Why is there aversion or distrust of
leadership?

Perhaps the answer lies in the scriptures cited above. In
everyday terms, leadership and its power is thought of in the
"gentile" sense. A leader is one who is over others, exerting
control, through whatever means society has given or allowed, to
direct the affairs of others. In a positive sense, this requires that
the leader be knowledgeable about the constituency involved,
and worthy of the trust granted by those who put her or him
in leadership. In a negative sense, the means used to exercise
power can be abusive and coercive, less concerned with the
rights of individual members of a community than on the "good
of the organization."

But Jesus tells us of a different type and style of leadership.
We will examine Christian leadership in this chapter: what it is
and how our beliefs about leadership affect the way our leaders
lead. Second, we will focus on the characteristics of servant-
leadership as a model for leadership in the Christian community.

Finally, we will reflect on our own feelings and talents with regard to leadership, especially within the parish.

Defining Leadership

Norman Shawchuck, in a practical booklet called *How To Be a More Effective Church Leader*, defines leadership as "the ability, and the activity of influencing people, and of shaping their behavior."[1] Notice two things about this definition: 1) leadership is a process, not merely a combination of personality traits; and 2) leadership does not always center on the appointed leader.

Four Views of Leadership

Social scientists have identified four approaches to understanding leadership: 1) leadership as a personality trait; 2) leadership as a relationship between leader and follower; 3) leadership as a relationship between leader and group; and 4) leadership as process of group interaction. Notice the similarity with Shawchuck's definition. Notice too that leadership is more a function of group interaction than a characteristic of the leader.

Leadership as Personality. How can a person be a more effective leader? One way might be to look at examples of people generally acknowledged as successful leaders. Attributes that have been successful for others perhaps could be developed in one's self.

Unfortunately, this theory has difficulties. How does one define success? What criteria are used to determine the success or failure of a leader? This theory also ignores the situation surrounding the exercise of leadership. For example, leadership in a board room can be far different from leadership on the bridge of a ship battling its way through a typhoon. Mother Teresa and George Washington are both acknowledged leaders, but how does one compare the two?

Of course the personality of the leader is important in the leadership process. But the most important contribution of a leader's personality seems to lie in how that leader's personality affects the group process. How a leader deals with setbacks or with criticism, for example, has a direct impact on the inner workings of the group. A leader can inspire by a movement of the head; a leader can demoralize a group with a flip remark. Personality is a key ingredient in the overall group dynamic, but it is not an individual guarantee of success.

Leader and Follower.   The second approach sees leadership as a relationship between leader and follower. The leader does not operate in a vacuum; others in the group are considered as well. An advantage of this "situational leadership" is to help the leader tailor his or her leadership style to the unique character of those being led. For example, working with a liturgy committee composed of adults will require a different style of leadership than teaching music to first-graders.

The strength of this approach is that leadership is seen as a function of interaction between leader and follower, with effectiveness being determined by the ability of the leader to adapt to the needs of a given situation. The shortcoming of this approach is that it still understands leadership as the exclusive function of the leader. In this case, the leader reacts to the situation and makes all the adjustments. "As this happens, we start to slip back into seeing the leader as the 'source' of the group's effectiveness. The contributions of other people become invisible."[2]

Leader and Group.   The third view of leadership focuses on the group involved. In this view people are no longer perceived as "leader" and "followers." The group has a communal identity, with functions to perform both internal and external to the group. The leader is more of a facilitator, encouraging group interaction, and sometimes even letting someone else "lead" the group. The leader does not, and in some cases should not, be in charge at all times. The leader influences the group, but does not dominate it.

The shortcoming of this approach is that the leader can still be perceived as distinct from the group. A fourth model may be discerned in which leadership is seen as a function of group interaction.

The Group and Its Leaders.   This last approach sees leadership "as the system of relationships through which a group acts effectively."[3] The strength of this approach lies in its realization that leadership occurs in far more subtle ways than previously imagined. If leadership is understood as "influencing others," this point becomes clear. People are influenced by many things and on many levels.

In this understanding of leadership, the leader can be the elderly man who attends daily Mass. The leader is the hospice volunteer who goes about her duties with so much love and care that others are infected by her witness. The leader is the "worker bee" on the liturgy committee who says little but does much—always working, always there, totally dedicated to the ministry at hand. In all these examples, if you asked the persons involved if they were "leaders," they would probably laugh and shake their heads. But they are all, in fact, leaders influencing the behavior of others by their own behavior.

Understood in this way, every group is composed of inter-dependent relationships.

> When there is a change in one relationship, all the other relationships are affected; the whole group is involved. Here the social science view reinforces a theology of the body: a group is a social body whose parts must interact harmoniously for its inner coordination and external effectiveness.[4]

Leadership in this view, therefore, is a process of the group, not something one person provides to the group. It is an interactive process, with all members taking a role. The role of the formal leader is quite different. Rather than an approach where the leader is the person who has all the answers and controls the group's agenda, the leader nurtures and sustains the group. It is in the light of this understanding that we can now move to an understanding of servant-leadership in the church.

Servant-Leadership in the Community of Faith

The scriptures show us servant-leadership as the model of Christian leadership. Leadership is equated with service to the community. Leadership is on behalf of the community, not for the personal gain of the leader. One who leads, serves. And one who serves, leads.

Robert K. Greenleaf cites a story by Herman Hesse called "Journey to the East."

> In this story we see a band of men on a mythical journey, probably Hesse's own journey. The central figure of the story is Leo who accompanies the party as the servant who does their menial chores, but who also sustains them with his spirit and his song. He is a person of extraordinary presence. All goes well until Leo disappears. Then the group falls into disarray and the journey is abandoned. They cannot make it without the servant Leo. The narrator, one of the party, after some years of wandering finds Leo and is taken into the Order that had sponsored the journey. There he discovers that Leo, whom he had known first as servant, was in fact the titular head of the Order, its guiding spirit, a great and noble leader.[5]

But what are the pastoral implications of servant-leadership in our parishes?

Pastoral Leadership

Christian servant-leadership demands that pastors, lay or clerical, keep two ingredients in balance: tasks and relationships. Charles J. Keating cites the following as task functions: initiating, regulating, informing, supporting, evaluating, and summarizing. These task functions need to be balanced with relationship functions such as encouraging, expressing feelings, harmonizing, compromising, facilitating, and setting standards.[6]

The servant-leader balances these two groups of function. James Dunning uses a circus image for the role of the pastor, that of a circus-master of a three-ring circus. He lists the gifts needed by those involved in pastoral work: self-confidence, listening and discerning, reconciling and peacemaking, vision, organization, patience, welcome, celebration, and enabling. Father Dunning explains his list this way:

In the midst of all this, pastors as circus masters need tremendous gifts: the gift of self-confidence so they are not threatened by performances they cannot render and talents they do not have; the gift of listening and discerning which helps other people discover their gifts; the gift of reconciling and peacemaking which heals the wounds of those who fall from the heights; the gift of vision which keeps them in touch with the total picture so that no ring in the circus dominates the show and excludes others with their talents; the gift of organization (not just administration) which helps them plan and facilitate with others the life of all the members; the gift of patience with the clowns and the gift of welcome to those who are still spectators; the gift of celebration when the entire community gathers to rejoice in their gifts and their care for each other. The new word is that the pastor is the great enabler of ministries, the great facilitator, who makes contributions to the community precisely by enabling the community to contribute to each other and to their God.[7]

Leadership and Power

No discussion of leadership would be complete without considering the relationship between leadership and power. The two are inseparable and our experience with the concept of power and those who exercise it tells us that power is used for good and for ill. Power within the framework of Christian leadership is a particularly sensitive issue, since much of our everyday experience with power seems unrelated, if not antithetical to Christian life itself. In this section, therefore, we will examine the nature of power, with specific reflections on the nature of power in the church.

The Nature of Power. Power is simply the ability to act effectively, to "get the job done," to do something. Such an ability works on every level of human existence. We speak of cars with powerful engines, storms with powerful winds. On a personal level we speak of powerful corporate executives, powerful works of art, powerful public speakers, or simply powerful personalities.

On the other hand, one who is powerless is unable to act effectively. The homeless, the elderly, the sick: all are powerless, in that they lack the ability to influence their situations. Likewise, the absence of power is experienced on every level of our lives, too. We speak of things being flat, useless, and lifeless. Sometimes we are just "helpless" in the face of some problem.

Power, then, is the ability to do something. But to do what, and why? And where does the power come from? It is here, in questions of motivation, intent, and authority, that we begin to see potential problems for the Christian leader. Once again we call upon the earlier distinction we made between "gentile" leadership and Christian leadership, only now we'll speak of "gentile" uses of power and Christian uses of power.

Gentile Uses of Power. The source of gentile power comes from the strength of the one in power over the ones dominated. For example, a gang exercises territorial control over a neighborhood because it is stronger and more physically intimidating than any one else in the neighborhood. A form of government that enforces its authority through the use of torture, intimidation, and fear is simply a gang in better clothes. The operative concepts of gentile power are strength and control.

The gentile leader, the "one who lords it over the rest," is one who will do whatever it takes to remain in a position of control. He or she will develop strong resources, both personal and economic, to use to stay in control. The goal is to remain "in power"; all else is secondary. The source of the gentile leader's authority is frequently his or her own power. A leader who assumes authority through a military coup or a corporate executive who fights her way to the top illustrates authority gained through personal power. Even in those cases in which authority is apparently given to a leader from another source, such as in political elections, such a transfer of authority comes about only through the strong personal influence and considerable resources of the one seeking power.

The Christian Leader and Power. The gentile leader is not necessarily a bad or selfish person. On the contrary, such a leader might have the noblest of goals and seek the betterment of those he or she leads. But what seems to distinguish the Christian leader from the gentile leader in the use of power is the Christian leader's recognition of God as the ultimate source of all power, which then affects the way in which power is exercised.

We believe with our Jewish and Christian ancestors that God is the source of all power. The point of the creation accounts in Genesis is to demonstrate dramatically the power of God over all creation. Jesus standing before Pilate, before the might of Rome, can say, "You would have no power over me at all if it had not been given you from above" (Jn 19:11).

The presence of Christ and the coming of the Spirit to the early communities of faith revealed the power of God given to the communities through the Spirit. These gifts, charisms, and powers were given freely to the members of these communities. Paul's witness to the many gifts but the one Spirit is a well-known example.

> There are many different gifts, but it is always the same Spirit; there are many different ways of serving, but it is always the same Lord. There are many different forms of activity, but in everybody it is the same God who is at work in them all. The particular manifestation of the Spirit granted to each one is to be used for the general good. To one is given from the Spirit the gift of utterance expressing wisdom; to another the gift of utterance expressing knowledge, in accordance with the same Spirit; to another, faith, from the same Spirit; and to another, the gifts of healing, through this one Spirit; to another, the working of miracles; to another, prophecy; to another, the power of distinguishing spirits; to one, the gift of different tongues and to another, the interpretation of tongues. But at work in all these is one and the same Spirit, distributing them at will to each individual (1 Cor 12:4–11).

Gradually, as the communities began to invest greater responsibility in their official leaders, things began to change. The charisms of teacher and prophet were given over to the early bishops, in addition to supervisory duties. Slowly, God's power within the community was perceived as coming to us through the mediation of official leaders. While church teaching has always maintained that God is the ultimate source of all power and authority in the church, the daily experience of church members is that official leaders of the church exercise power in God's name. And so we come to the source of conflict—the danger that church leaders, perhaps with the best of intentions but human nonetheless, might exercise "gentile" leadership rather than truly Christian leadership.

The exercise of power, as a particular component of leadership, cannot be as easily distinguished in practice as our discussion might suggest. There are elements of gentile uses of power in the daily exercise of ecclesiastical leadership just as there can be elements of Christian uses of power in secular life. In our imperfect world, some "Christian" leaders (lay and ordained) misuse their authority and attempt to coerce and control. Decisions are made and actions performed that seek to preserve the status quo more than to serve the just needs of the community. The challenge for Christian leaders is to keep Jesus' mandate for servant leadership pre-eminent in the exercise of power. When conflicts arise, how are they resolved? Jesus did not come to sanctify the status quo: If something needed to be changed, he took action to change it. Preservation of structures for control was not on his agenda.

The challenge, then, to all Christian leaders is to foster true servant (that is, noncontrolling) leadership. The key characteristic of the servant is that he or she does not *control* anything or anyone. Gifts of leadership must be exercised without falling into the trap of gentile leadership. What we are about is God's work, not doing our own work and using the name of God as our authority: that is blasphemous. Power is God's gift to the community to "get the job done." Just as leadership is a function of the entire community, so too is that community empowered through the grace of God. It is important that the community realize its power, and it is especially important that the Christian leader understand and be unafraid of the power given to that community. Power is the Spirit's way of enabling us to continue the work of Christ in proclaiming the coming of the kingdom.

SUMMARY

Leadership, understood properly as a process involving all members of a group, is part of our Christian vocation of service. Christians are called to stand up for what they believe and to take responsibility for their actions. Christian leadership is a process of servanthood, with those entrusted with special leadership roles at the service of the rest. Through the power of the Spirit, the Christian community is gifted with the talents and abilities necessary for the community to prosper; the leader's task is to recognize, encourage, and support them.

QUESTIONS FOR REFLECTION

How is leadership perceived in various parts of your life: your family, your job, your church?

How is leadership exercised in those environments?

How do you lead? Do you have a role model for leadership: a boss, relative, pastor, or friend?

Who are the leaders of your parish? In other words, who are the people who seem to influence others the most? How does this list compare with a listing of parish staff?

How well is every member of the parish able to exercise his or her leadership, and how willing are they to do it?

FOR FURTHER READING

I strongly urge anyone interested in understanding leadership—personal leadership and church leadership—to use Dr. Shawchuck's book, *How To Be a More Effective Church Leader.* The author describes a seven-step approach to analyzing and applying one's approaches to leadership. It is a practical little workbook that will give you invaluable insights into yourself as a leader.

NOTES

[1] Norman Shawchuck, *How To Be a More Effective Church Leader* (Irvine, CA: Spiritual Growth Resources, 1986), p. 6.

[2] James D. Whitehead and Evelyn Eaton Whitehead, *The Emerging Laity: Returning Leadership to the Community of Faith* (New York: Doubleday, 1986), p. 72.

[3] Ibid., p. 74.

[4] Ibid., p. 75.

[5] Robert K. Greenleaf, *Servant Leadership: A Journey Into the Nature of Legitimate Power and Greatness* (Mahwah, NJ: Paulist Press, 1977), p. 7.

[6] Charles J. Keating, *The Leadership Book* (Mahwah, NJ: Paulist Press, 1978), pp. 13–15.

[7] James B. Dunning, *Ministries: Sharing God's Gifts* (Winona, MN: St. Mary's Press, 1980 (Third printing, 1985), pp. 69–70.

CHAPTER 4

Pastoral Planning

INTRODUCTION

Pastoral planning is the process that turns the community's vision into reality, and it is the responsibility of every member of the parish. It begins with a community's view of itself and the world in which it exists. This assessment surfaces needs, identifies gifts and resources, and provides the impetus and the raw data to proceed. The community can now "see" itself as it is and begin to "see" where the Lord is leading it. Now the mission is to translate this vision into a vibrant reality.

The lay leader can play many roles in this process. At one end of the spectrum is the member of the parish with no formal leadership function but whose imput is just as important as the parish council president's. As discussed in chapter three, all baptized members of the parish share in its leadership and are responsible for the life of the parish. At the other end of the spectrum is the lay leader who is functioning as a lay administrator of a parish in the absence of a resident pastor. Regardless of the position the lay leader is in, pastoral planning should be of prime concern.

This chapter presents one approach to pastoral planning. Pastoral planning is dependent on many things: the nature and needs of the unique faith community, the policies and procedures of the deanery and diocese, and the resources available to you. But there are common elements at work in developing a pastoral plan. After some initial reflections, we will examine those elements.

Planning in a World of Change

The church exists in a world of change. One of the goals of Vatican II was to enable the universal church to deal with the complexities of this ever-changing world. No one really likes change, but most people are used to it in their professional and

49

private lives. Many, however, are not used to a changing church, even though our history shows us to be a church of change and adaptation. Pope John XXIII saw that the church had to learn to live with change, to carry the message of Christ forward into the contemporary world.

The church is real people living in a real world. We are the light of the world and the salt of the earth. As the people of God we are meant to be the leaven for transforming the world.

Planning is how we cope with change, whether that change comes as a surprise or is a goal we consciously work to bring about. We plan for most things in life. We have financial plans, operational plans, training plans, business plans, travel plans, and flight plans. All of our plans help us cope with the changes which may happen or which we hope will happen. So it is with pastoral planning. A good pastoral plan helps us deal with the contingencies and goals of the future.

Pastoral Planning and Church Renewal

The Diocese of Portland, Maine, through its Office of Pastoral Planning, publishes a document entitled *The Parish Council*. The information contained in this slim volume is of much broader scope than its title indicates. It provides a good background on the elements of pastoral planning as well as specific policy guidelines for pastoral planning in the diocese. The process is offered as a practical, comprehensive model; pertinent forms and other documentation from this process are provided in appendix B.

The Parish Council makes an important statement concerning pastoral planning:

> If a "methodical planning process" were the only contribution of Pastoral Planning, it would already be worth our effort; but there is much more. Let us look at 4 elements which Pastoral Planning introduces into the Church and we will quickly realize that in addition to being a "skill", it is also an effective method of implementing some of the most important elements of the

Second Vatican Council (1962–1965) on Church renewal (p. 28).

The four elements—regarded as indispensable areas of renewal in the church—are purposes, shared responsibility, accountability, and direction. By focusing on purposes, we are able to identify our vision: what we are about as the people of God, the church of Christ. By sharing responsibility for the tasks and mission of the church, we help each other realize our call to discipleship. Accountability shows us the importance of our contributions and the depth of our stewardship. The element of direction energizes our vision, enabling us to move forward on our journey. These four elements can be the catalyst for true renewal in the church. "Pastoral planning," according to the document, "is one way—a proven method—for bringing these conditions about."

Pastoral Planning and the Local Church

Many dioceses have guidelines for parish pastoral planning, thus enabling the diocese to acquire consistent data from its parishes and to formulate a diocesan pastoral plan. If you are part of a parish pastoral team without a full-time resident pastor, you should check with the priest who is assigned as your coordinator, the local dean, or with the chancery office for more information. The dean is most important to you, especially if you are in a larger diocese. Most dioceses are subdivided into a number of smaller administrative units known as deaneries. The function of the dean (usually an experienced pastor in the region) is to coordinate various aspects of diocesan policy for the bishop. In some cases, for example, the parish pastoral plan is submitted to the dean before it goes to the diocese.

Your community is not planning in a vacuum. The diocese and deanery are your partners in planning, with resources and support to assist the parish pastoral team. The pattern of pastoral planning proposed below is based in large part on the guidance and assistance provided by the Diocese of Portland, Maine. I am most grateful to Bishop Edward O'Leary (now retired) for permission to present this model to you.

The Pastoral Council

All members of the community are responsible for the pastoral planning process. Nonetheless, a small cadre of the community should be identified to coordinate the pastoral plan. This may be the full parish council, or a subcommittee may be set up specifically to handle the plan. For convenience sake, we shall refer to this group simply as the "pastoral council."

The primary purpose of the pastoral council is to plan the various aspects of parish life. The council grows from the community of faith to serve the community of faith. Given the nature of the council and the gifts of its membership, it should serve as a witness to the rest of the community. This group will pray and work together, and by so doing demonstrate to the rest of the community what a community of faith can and should be. In other words, the pastoral council should be a spiritual as well as an administrative body.

The pastoral council should be concerned with every aspect of community life. So, in addition to the council president, secretary, and pastor, several standing organizations need to be established. Our model proposes six standing commissions to encompass the community. (See appendix B, pp. 96–98.) They are:

- Church Life Commission
- Worship and Spirituality Commission
- Religious Education Commission
- Social Justice and Peace Commission
- Family Life Commission
- Finance and Administration Commission

Each commission can include committees as needed for specific programs. For example, the Religious Education Commission might include committees on adult catechesis, continuing education for ministers, and CCD. The Social Justice and Peace Commission might have committees on right to life, legislative network, and food pantry. Depending on the size of the community, each committee would have a chairperson and each commission a commissioner. This is a comprehensive model.

The Council and the Pastoral Plan

The pastoral council has a massive agenda centered on two complementary concerns. First, what needs to be done in, for, and by the community in the short term? The council will need to address issues which require immediate action, such as recommended personnel actions or to give approval to the CCD textbook purchase order. The second concern is the long-range aspect of pastoral planning. While the rest of this chapter focuses on the long-range activity of the council, that is not meant to downplay its more short-term function.

Most pastoral plans are updated annually, so the first thing to find out is when this update is due to the chancery (the bishop's office). What intermediate steps are expected or required? If the plan is due to the bishop on July 1, the dean may wish to review it the previous month. With this information, you can begin scheduling the planning agenda. We'll have more to say about that later.

Obtain copies of previous pastoral plans. If there are none, find a copy of another parish's previous plans that have been approved. This will give the council a good starting point.

The Nine Steps of Pastoral Planning

As found in the Diocese of Portland, Maine model, here are the nine steps of pastoral planning:

> Purposes—areas of concern
> Responsibilities
> Basic Research
> Ongoing Programs
> Setting Goals
> Goal Selection
> Objectives
> Pastoral Plan
> Evaluation

Step One: Purposes—Areas of Concern. The basic question to be answered is: "Why do we exist?" This is the point from which everything else flows. "Because this is why we exist, we should do _____." As the handbook describing the model states, "A purpose should be inspiring and non-specific. It should be broad and idealistic. It should not be measurable, for it has no terminal point; it is open-ended."

This first step also asks you to develop your "areas of concern." These areas are the extensions of the purposes of the parish. If the purposes are stated in idealistic terms, the areas of concern begin to concretize them. The six areas of concern developed by the church in Portland, Maine correspond to the six commissions of the pastoral council already discussed.

Step Two: Responsibilities. The purpose of this step is to make sure things don't fall through the cracks. Specific responsibilities should be developed for the pastoral staff, the parish council, and each of the commissions.

Step Three: Basic Research. The point of the planning process is to reflect the vision, needs, and dreams of the entire community of faith, not merely those of the pastoral staff and council. Therefore it is essential that adequate research be done on each member of the parish. This is a stupendous task, even in a small parish, but it must be done.

First, data must be collected on the local community in which the parish is located. Three areas need to be explored: 1) Demographic questions: What is the population of the area; is the population expected to grow, decline, or shift in some way; what is the age distribution of the population? 2) Social questions: What is the educational level of the population; what is the average length of residence in the community; what types of civic and fraternal organizations are present? 3) Economic questions: What is the average family income; is there any new industry; has industry moved away? Sources for these data are the Board of Education, the Census Bureau, the library, and perhaps the state government.

Now situate your parish within this context. Appendix B (pp. 106–107) contains another extract from *The Parish Council* that gives a useful breakdown of the data desired. You may determine that some of this data is not needed, or that other information is needed; these are merely suggestions. Record your findings on a form such as the one provided in appendix B (p. 108).

Once you have acquired the data, each commission can do its own analysis and report to the full council. For example, if the population is expected to increase sharply over the next year because of construction of a new factory, every area of the parish will be affected. More Catholics will be coming into the area, placing greater demand on school/educational programs. With the data, the commissions and the council can assess the adequacy of current programs to meet these demands.

Step Four: Ongoing Programs. In this step what is happening now is reported. A listing of the major programs already in place should be done; for example, "CCD program for grades K - 12" or "monthly parish newsletter." This list is just a snapshot; no great descriptions are needed. Keep it simple!

Step Five: Identifying Goals. Up to this point you have been developing a picture of your parish in the present. Now you are ready to look to the future by identifying possible goals and identifying the objectives needed to achieve them.

In the Portland model, a goal is defined with the question: "Where do we want to be in five years?" Compare goals with purposes. Where purposes are open-ended and abstract, goals are concrete and measurable. Being a sailor, I found the language from the handbook on this point particularly apt: Goals are five-year targets which "are rarely attained, in fact, for they can be updated yearly; they serve more as a star serves to guide a mariner—he aims for it and is guided by it but never attains it."

This step is best accomplished by each commission brainstorming its own goals, followed by another brainstorming session in full council. There is no judgment to be made here: selection of goals is the next step. You simply want to identify the possible goals of your parish. Given your purposes, responsibilities, the basic research and ongoing problems, where might you want to be in five years? (See appendix B, p. 111.)

Step Six: Goal Selection. In Irving Stone's biographical novel *The Agony and the Ecstasy*, he describes Michelangelo as being able to approach a solid slab of marble and see the shape of the figure within it; the process was one of removing the excess marble from around it to set it free. That is what this step is all about.

In brainstorming, you probably generated far more goals than you could possibly attain. It is time now to focus on those goals that correspond to the greatest needs and for which you have or can acquire sufficient resources to realize the goals. More important, this is the step in which your parish's vision of the future can take shape. The decisions made in this step are crucial, for they reflect the dedication and consistency of your parish. Which goals best reflect your parish's vision?

The focus must be on the needs and the resources available (or attainable) to meet those needs. Otherwise you run the risk of selecting unrealistic goals. Even Michelangelo needed money and tools to free his vision from the marble.

Step Seven: Objectives. If purposes answer the question "Why?", goals answer the question "What?" and objectives answer the question "How?". See appendix B (pp. 112–114) for suggestions on developing one-year objectives and for articulating the selected goals and the objectives to meet them.

Step Eight: The Pastoral Plan. Once your goals and objectives have been voted on and approved, you are ready to assemble the plan. Put the various forms together—purposes, responsibilities, ongoing programs, goals, and objectives—and you're almost there! The pastor, parish council president, and bishop all sign the final document, your pastoral plan for the coming year. Put a cover sheet on the document (See appendix B, p. 115.) and you're ready to submit it to the bishop and publish it throughout the parish. It's important that the entire parish be made aware of the plan and its contents, so distribute it as widely as possible.

Step Nine: Evaluation. This step is probably the most important. Now you have to evaluate how well your plan is followed and what adjustments, additions, or deletions need to be made for the next planning cycle. This process can be very fulfilling as you see your vision being realized. You may also find that your goals were not really goals, but objectives following from unnamed goals. Nevertheless, your parish will benefit and grow. It is best to conduct this review about nine months into the year of the pastoral plan. In Portland, this time of self-evaluation by the local parish was followed by a deanery review just prior to beginning the next planning cycle. See appendix B (p. 116) for suggestions on evaluating your pastoral plan.

Scheduling

It is recommended that the pastoral planning effort begin in March in order to submit your final plan by July 1. This gives you an indication of the work involved. Find a variety of ways to get many people involved. While the bulk of the work will be done by committees and the commissions, a parish-wide meeting should be held, to which everyone is invited. That is the time to explain the process and answer any questions. Ask for the prayers of the parish, and solicit the help of any who may be interested.

Don't expect to get this all done during normal parish council meetings! Other meetings will be needed by various subcommittees which can then report their findings to the commissions or the full council for approval. Remember that the pastoral plan is a vision and a dream that reflects the deepest realities of your parish. It should not be done haphazardly.

SUMMARY

The work of pastoral planning is both frustrating and fulfilling. Keep in mind that your parish is the people of God, and the work you are about is God's work. You are proclaiming to yourselves and to the world who you are and how you intend to live out this reality in your daily lives. It is a sublime and awesome task. After a marathon session of haggling over objectives, after battling for days for a new priority in the budget, after dozens of dumb remarks made in frustration and fatigue, pull together and pray. Pray for the wisdom, courage, and serenity that is yours for the asking. Make the Lord a member of your pastoral council!

QUESTIONS FOR REFLECTION

How can the most people be encouraged to participate in the pastoral planning process?

If you were the sole planner for your parish, what would your pastoral plan look like?

If you could select only one thing to work on in the parish, what would it be? (In other words, what do you think the parish's number-one priority should be?)

FOR FURTHER READING

Any number of good resources are available for project planning, far too many to enumerate here. Actually, background reading in this area might be more of a hindrance than a help. What is most important are the vision and dreams of the parish, and for that you need prayer, faith, prayer, hope, prayer, and love. Documenting them will require more of the same. Remember two important things. First, your pastoral council is made up of volunteers who will not necessarily be experienced project managers. You will need a plan that is straightforward and easy to implement. Second, the nature of the parish is more than the sum of its members. As the council narrows its focus to deal with the fine details of the plan, keep the visionary statement of purpose in mind.

CHAPTER 5

The Lay Leader and Public Prayer

INTRODUCTION

Just as individual prayer is indispensable to the life of the Christian, so public prayer is indispensable to the life of the Christian community. But the notion of leading public prayer is something most lay persons have never had to face. In our tradition that has been the province of priests and religious.

We have already seen that lay leaders fulfill a variety of functions in the community. In some cases, lay leadership may include presiding at public prayer. In other cases, in which ordained leadership is available, the lay leader may still serve as presider in prayer groups or liturgies of the word when the priest or deacons cannot be present. In situations in which lay leaders are serving on a pastoral team without ordained leadership, they may be responsible for leading the public prayer of the entire community.

The purpose of this chapter is to examine the types of public prayer lay leaders may be responsible for as well as some reflections on the role of the lay presider. In order to consider as many options as possible, we will consider the range of options in public prayer available to a lay-led parish.

Range of Public Prayer

There are many types of public prayer, ranging from devotions such as the rosary or stations of the cross to the highest form of public worship, the celebration of the eucharist. With the exception of the eucharist, lay leaders can preside over a diverse community prayer life centered on the eucharist.

The basic dynamic of our life of faith is simple: God calls and we respond. That is the basic rule of the covenant: "I will be your God and you will be my people." God calls through the word, the word as proclaimed throughout the history of salvation, the word as lived in Jesus the Christ, the word as lived in the community of faith. From the earliest days of our tradition, we covenant people have come together to "gather the folks, break the bread, and tell the stories."[1] Our public prayer, therefore, is centered on the presence of God in our midst, calling us all to a renewed sense of belonging, a renewed sense of covenant, a renewed sense of response to God's call.

Some communities that gather for public prayer choose a liturgy not patterned on the eucharistic celebration. This is done deliberately for two excellent reasons. First, there is concern that a celebration that is "Mass-like" will be confusing to the assembly, that a liturgy of the word followed by a Rite of Communion using hosts consecrated at a previous Mass will be confused with a Mass. Second, there is a sense that, if the eucharist cannot be celebrated because no priest is present, the eucharist *should* be missed, focusing our attention on the fact that the celebration of eucharist is more than receiving communion, that it is the entire action of the eucharistic assembly we celebrate at Mass. Therefore, in some communities, public prayer in the absence of a priest takes alternate forms such as the liturgy of the hours, or a liturgy of the word (without a Rite of Communion).

In other communities, the weekly liturgy is deliberately patterned after the Mass, also for good reasons. First, a liturgy of the word followed by the Rite of Communion follows a pattern of public prayer that is familiar to the assembly. Because the eucharist is the center of our public prayer, these communities feel that all public prayer should be as "eucharistic" (i. e., contain as many eucharistic elements) as possible. In such communities, the liturgy follows the format provided in the sacramentary for Mass, with the exception of the eucharistic prayer: the introductory rites, liturgy of the word, communion rite, and closing rites are all included.

The choice to be made lies with the community involved. In some dioceses, the bishop has provided specific instruction on how he wants lay-led worship services to be conducted. The National Conference of Catholic Bishops has approved a Rite for Sunday Worship Without a Priest for use throughout the United

States. Canada has had two such rites in use for some time. All of these follow what I shall refer to as the "eucharistic model" of liturgy of the word coupled with a Rite of Communion.

Regardless of the model adopted, the eucharist is the center of our public prayer because it is the celebration of God's presence among us. The Mass is the best and highest expression of this presence, but it is not the only way. We celebrate God's presence in the word and in each other whenever we gather as God's people. That is the central meaning of the sign of the assembly. "For where two or three meet in my name, I am there among them" (Mt 18:20).

With this in mind, consider these words of introduction to the *Ritual For Lay Presiders*, published and approved by the Western Liturgical Conference of Canada (Archdiocese of Regina):

It is essential to the life of the Catholic church that those initiated into the faith be called together on the Lord's Day. This is true at all times, whether or not the bishop is among them to preside, whether or not there are priests in the place of the bishop. The Lord's Day is best celebrated with the full eucharist; when a community has such a possibility, it is indeed blessed and should be a blessing to others.

Not all communities can have a Sunday eucharist presided over by a bishop or priest: all across the world, more and more communities find themselves with fewer occasions when a bishop or priest is present to proclaim the eucharistic Prayer, and lead the assembly into the sacred covenant in Christ's body and blood. For some Catholics, this is an altogether new experience: many years of daily and Sunday Mass have suddenly given way to less frequent or even infrequent celebrations led by a priest.

The local community must continue to gather, nonetheless. It must resist the facile solution, namely, to abandon its own roots and travel several or even many miles to join another community. The faith is lived in the local community: it is there that it should be celebrated, and not elsewhere . . . . [2]

The 1983 revised *Code of Canon Law* not only permits but encourages such gatherings of the assembly:

> If because of lack of a sacred minister or for other grave cause participation in the celebration of the Eucharist is impossible, it is specially recommended that the faithful take part in the liturgy of the word . . . . [3]

Getting Started

Let's assume you have never presided at public prayer, and you're trying to get organized for your first community celebration of the word. Let's also assume that you have a place of repose for the hosts consecrated at a previous Mass which your community will share in a Rite of Communion. Where do you begin?

For many in your community this will be the first time they've gathered for this type of service, and they will be confused. You need to gather a group who can plan the liturgy well and eliminate this confusion. The role of this team is to coordinate and plan all aspects of the liturgy: ministers of hospitality, music, and environment, as well as ministers of the word and eucharist.

Second, you need an outline to follow. To illustrate, let's assume you're following the "eucharistic model." Four resources are critical: the newly approved rite (for dioceses in the United States), a sacramentary, a lectionary, and an ordo.

The sacramentary is the book the presider uses in the liturgy. It contains all the prayers you will need for your celebration. It also contains useful information about how to celebrate the service. You should take some time to become familiar and comfortable with the sacramentary, including the General Instruction to the Roman Missal (GIRM—known affectionately as the "germ") and the foreword. There is more in the sacramentary than you'll need for the liturgy of the word and the communion service, but it will give you a good "feel" for what the celebration is all about. With the introduction of the rite by the NCCB, the sacramentary will provide a wealth of background for your preparation and worship.

The lectionary contains the readings to be proclaimed during the liturgy of the word. Here again, there is much useful information beyond the readings themselves. Note that each reading is numbered. This is to help you refer to a reading quickly and easily. One of the liturgical changes brought about by Vatican II was to broaden the use of scripture in our worship. For this reason, a three-year cycle was established for Sunday readings, and a two-year cycle for weekday readings. To plan, you will need to know which cycle you're in. For example, there are three sets of readings for each Sunday of the year. Which ones do you use? The readings are numbered independently of the cycle, so if the ordo tells you the reading is number 235, you can find it easily and know that you're in the right cycle.

The ordo contains everything you need to know about setting up for the day's celebration. It's sort of a liturgical crib sheet that tells you what the celebration is, what liturgical color is used, what the readings are (by lectionary number), and any special prayers that need to be said. Published annually, each diocese has its own. The information in the ordo can be obtained in other places, although usually not in as complete a form. Several companies publish desk and pocket calendars that contain much of the same information.

Always let the scripture readings set the tone and theme of your public prayer service. The word forms the center of the prayer, and our focus as the body of Christ is found in the proclamation. Don't fall into the trap of "theme" celebrations (friendship, happiness, the first day of Spring), unless the message of the word clearly leads to the theme.

Presiding at Public Prayer

What is involved in presiding at public prayer? Dolly Sokol has written a series of articles in *Liturgy 80* (published by the Office of Divine Worship of the Archdiocese of Chicago) entitled "Lay Leaders of Prayer." These excellent articles provide a superb resource for all lay presiders.

In her first article, Sokol offers some thoughts on the qualities expected in lay presiders, and attitudes people have about what makes good presiding. She describes four "qualities of lay presiders." (They could be applied to ordained presiders as well.) 1) They must be persons of deep faith in Jesus Christ. Presiding is not the performance of an actor on stage; it is public articulation of belief rooted in the person of the presider which is shared with the rest of the community. 2) Presiders must remember that they are servants of the community: this is not the place for a solo profession of faith. The presider needs to "enable the prayer of God's people."[4] 3) Public prayer must grow out of private prayer. We must be on fire to enflame others. 4) Lay presiders must be willing to continue to learn and discover. This means a willingness to work hard in preparation for presiding. Lay presiding is a whole new aspect of ministry, and the only way to learn it is to practice.

Based on her experience with lay-presider workshops, Sokol cites the following observations from her students: 1) People look for prayerfulness in presiders, a sense that they are participating in a sacred act. This is reflected in the way they dress, the way they stand and move, and how prepared they are. This must be balanced, however, by a sense of the community, being careful not to be rigid or aloof. 2) Conversely, people respond negatively when there is too much folksiness and no sense of the sacred. 3) People want to sense the presider is with them in prayer. When you pray the creed, do you pray along with the people, or do stop after beginning, "We believe in one God..."? 4) Lastly, presiders should respect the assembly and the other ministers.

Let's consider a list of skills a presider should possess. As Sokol points out, some of these can be acquired through practice; others come naturally to some people:

- clear articulation, sufficient volume, and comfortable pitch.
- good oral interpretation skills. (Know what you're saying and how to say it to convey the meaning.)
- ability to move comfortably and gracefully.
- ability to focus attention appropriately. (Where do you look during communal prayer? during the readings?)
- ability to "pace" the rite, to sense the "rhythm" of worship.

- ability to coordinate the other ministries smoothly.

Presiding: A Pastoral Perspective

The community expects certain things from its public prayer. It expects a sense of the sacred, of Christ's presence in its midst. It expects integrity and honesty on the part of its ministers. The assembly is more than the sum of its individual members: it is the body of Christ. The shape, tone, and texture of this experience is influenced greatly by the presider.

When we began our lay-led prayer services, one of our concerns was that we didn't want to confuse people by what we were doing. The model we chose was the "eucharistic model," primarily because we didn't realize we could substitute something else, but also because the community wanted to be able to receive communion as part of the celebration. We didn't want to send wrong signals that we were "playing priest" and trying to "say Mass." Since I was going to preside, I especially wanted to make sure that people could recognize from the beginning that what we were doing was a legitimate and solemn celebration. Let me give two examples of how we tried to do that.

It was the practice of the nearest parish to have their extraordinary ministers of communion wear albs when doing their ministry. In addition, they were present in the sanctuary throughout the liturgy of the word. Many newcomers to the parish thought that they were priest-concelebrants. Although this was the tradition in the area, we decided that I would not wear an alb when presiding in our community, even though most people would have accepted it. I wanted to make clear that what I was doing was by right of baptism, and I didn't want to cloud the issue by communicating that only people in vestments can approach the altar.

Second, I followed the rites given in the sacramentary carefully, especially in the beginning. We used various options, but I wanted people to have a sense of the familiar in the pacing and rhythm of the rite. (Now, lay presiders have the NCCB Rite, and the sacramentary is not needed.) With sufficient preparation, the movements, gestures, and words of the rite can become the natural expressions of the presider.

Presiding and Preaching

One of the most thrilling and awesome experiences you can have is sharing the word of God with your community. No matter what your experience in public speaking, nothing can prepare you for the experience of your first homily. In general, homilies are restricted to the ordained only during Mass; during a liturgy of the word, anyone may offer a shared reflection, or homily, on the scripture.

I can't remember what I said at my first homily, but I remember the experience. As everyone sat down after the gospel, and I remained standing, I suddenly realized what an awesome responsibility this was. This was no class in religious education: this was a public reflection on the word of God. Could I do it? Could I offer the community something worthwhile, or would it all sound trite, shallow, or (pardon the overworked expression) irrelevant? My first feelings were of humility and a deep sense of responsibility to the community. But the experience taught me an invaluable lesson. This wasn't my homily. I was sharing what I believed God was saying to me in the readings. This was God's homily. I was only the messenger, not the originator of the message. Before a priest or deacon proclaims the gospel, he offers a short prayer: "Almighty God, cleanse my heart and my lips that I may worthily proclaim your gospel." It's a good prayer for the lay presider as well.

Lastly, I again refer you to the *Ritual For Lay Presiders*. The words of encouragement given in the introductory comments concerning preaching by lay presiders are excellent:

> Be assured, everyone wants to hear what the Spirit says to you: all want to be lifted up, given new hope. Trust in God: it is a continuance of Christ's work that you are undertaking. Everyone wants you to succeed.[5]

Pray - Prepare - Practice - Persevere

Before moving on to other examples of public prayer, let's offer some concluding remarks on presiding, especially at the community's Sunday liturgy of the word and communion service.

Prayer is the cornerstone of all life and ministry. If your ministry includes presiding, you must be intense in your prayer. Your relationship with God and your ability to communicate with God, even in the toughest of times, will be reflected in your presiding. People don't respect phonies, and they especially don't want phonies for leaders of public prayer. We can accept sinners and people who are struggling to live a life of faith; the experiences of sin and struggle make us equal in the sight of God. But phonies, people who put on a false show of religiosity while living only for themselves, are unacceptable. Prayer, that constant reaching out for God, will keep us honest and oriented toward the Lord.

Preparation and practice are the hallmarks of a professional in any public arena. No one can become a leader of public prayer without preparation and practice. There is no excuse for fumbling through the pages of the rite or the lectionary. Your community should have a team dedicated to preparing your liturgies. You should help each other prepare and practice what you've planned. Be professional in your ministry.

Lastly, persevere. No one expects your first homily to be a candidate for the Bishop Sheen Preaching Award. Nor does anyone expect your communal prayer to be choreographed like the Joffrey Ballet. What people do expect are honesty and integrity.

Other Forms of Public Prayer

Much of what we've discussed in this chapter applies to all forms of public prayer. What I hope to do now is indicate the variety of public prayer available to your community. For convenience, I will distinguish between sacramental prayer and devotional prayer. I want to distinguish public prayer, which is more related to the sacraments, from prayer that is more devotional.

As canon law states, lay leaders can be deputed to preside over a variety of sacramental prayer services in the absence of a priest. We've already discussed the liturgy of the word and the

Rite of Communion Outside Mass. Also in this category would be the Rite of Baptism, penitential services (not the sacrament of reconciliation), witnessing of marriages, and praying for the sick, including taking *viaticum* to the sick and infirm of the community. These services must be coordinated and approved by your priest supervisor or bishop.

In the "devotional" category I would include charismatic prayer groups, rosary services, exposition of the Blessed Sacrament (without benediction, which is reserved to priests or deacons), public novenas, bible sharing groups, and any other services your community finds meaningful. In these cases, you would not expect to be the presider, although you could. Notice that the minister for exposition and reposition of the Blessed Sacrament is to be a duly-appointed extraordinary minister of the eucharist.

SUMMARY

The public prayer life of your community can be as varied and diverse as your imagination and canon law allow. The public prayer life of the community is probably the most visible sign of your covenant faith. It demands and deserves all the energy, time, and professionalism the entire community can give to it. Even though you cannot celebrate the eucharist without a priest or bishop, your community can celebrate the presence of God in its midst.

QUESTIONS FOR REFLECTION

What makes a good presider? We looked at Dolly Sokol's list; now make your own. Reflect on liturgies you've participated in and list what you remember about the presider. What made the most impact on you? What touched a responsive chord in you and what turned you cold? Is there a pattern to what you've observed?

What about other elements of public worship? What enhances or detracts from liturgy? How is music handled, and how is the worship space decorated and prepared for prayer?

FOR FURTHER READING

There are a variety of homiletic aids available. I found the following ones useful for me. Probably the best one-volume reference book for homilists is Reginald Fuller's classic text, *Preaching the Lectionary*, which offers brief observations about each reading in each cycle and includes some recommendations for the homilist. If you're really mystified by a text and want to do some research into it, try the *Jerome Biblical Commentary*. It is a scholarly work, extraordinarily thorough, and expensive—probably the best one-volume bible commentary available.

Two other practical and useful books on public worship are Aidan Kavanagh's *Elements of Rite* and and O. C. Edwards' *Elements of Homiletic*.

NOTES

[1] John Shea, *Stories of God: An Unauthorized Biography* (Chicago: Thomas More Press, 1978), p. 8.

[2] *Ritual For Lay Presiders*, published by the Western Liturgical Conference of Canada, Regina, Saskatchewan, Canada, 1984, p. i.

[3] Canon 1248, #2. For the complete text, see Appendix A.

[4] Dolly Sokol, "Lay Leaders of Prayer," *Liturgy* 80, Volume 18, No. 8, p. 10.

[5] *Ritual*, p. vii.

A Pastoral Potpourri

INTRODUCTION

Throughout these reflections I've tried to steer you toward resources that might prove helpful. We've covered a number of topics of interest to lay leaders, but this little book is a resource guide, not a compendium. All a guide can do is point the way; the journey you take will depend on factors beyond the scope of this work. What I'd like to do now is provide an annotated bibliography for the lay pastor. In this way, I can point you to resources on a wide variety of issues, including some we have not covered in the other chapters. Details are provided in the bibliography that follows.

Organizational Resources

One of your primary sources is the diocese in which you're working. If you are in a parish without ordained leadership, another local priest can help you get started. But the chancery organization will provide you with policy guidance, diocesan forms for record-keeping, and training programs for lectors, special ministers of the eucharist, catechists, and other ministers. Most dioceses have offices of pastoral planning; for just about anything you're doing within your community, there is a diocesan counterpart.

The local dean and other local pastors can offer much from their experience, and some programs, such as CCD or ministerial training, can be combined to be more effective.

Local or regional colleges and universities can assist by providing guest speakers on a variety of topics. Recent graduates and graduate students are often looking for employment and make good candidates for ministries to youth, music, catechetics, and others. Scour the local area for resources that may be unique to your area. And don't forget the offices of the chancery.

Building Up the Church

You should be aware of the documents of Vatican II, especially those that deal with the nature of the church and the role of the laity. We touched on *The Dogmatic Constitution on the Church* in chapter one. Richard McBrien gives a good overview of all the documents in Chapter 19 ("The Church of the Second Vatican Council") of his book *Catholicism*. The documents themselves are available in various editions. One good edition is a two-volume paperback set that contains not only the original sixteen documents of Vatican II but assorted postconciliar documents as well.

In *The Pastoral Associate and the Lay Pastor*, Mary Moisson Chandler offers a good overview of lay pastoral ministry and a particularly useful treatment of the canons pertaining to lay pastoral ministry. She also suggests job descriptions and lists qualifications for the positions of "pastoral associate" and "lay pastor." Leonard Doohan's books, *The Lay-Centered Church* and *Laity's Mission in the Local Church*, are well done, but a bit more theological in tone than Chandler's book. Delores Leckey, the Executive Director of the U. S. Bishops' Committee on the Laity, has written *Laity Stirring the Church: Prophetic Questions*, which is very enlightening across a spectrum of issues. Her office has also put together *To Build and Be Church: Lay Ministry Resource Packet* which contains eighteen articles addressing a wide variety of lay ministry issues.

I would also include the revised *Code of Canon Law*. The new *Code* offers a significant new perspective on the role of the laity. Many programs (such as the Diocese of Little Rock's "Priestless Sundays") and authors (such as Mary Moisson Chandler in *Pastoral Associates and Lay Pastors*) have based their work solidly in the documents of Vatican II and the revised *Code*. A particularly useful edition is *The Code of Canon Law: A Text and Commentary* commissioned by the Canon Law Society of America.

Ministry

Father Bill Bausch's trilogy *The Christian Parish*, *Ministry: Traditions, Tensions, Transitions*, and *Take Heart, Father* is a remarkable view of the church today and vision of the church of the future. The books by James D. Whitehead and Evelyn Eaton Whitehead offer a solid foundation in the notion of service and leadership in the Christian community. Andrew Greeley, Mary Durkin, David Tracy, John Shea, and William McCready teamed up on *Parish, Priest and People*, stressing the centrality of the parish in the continuing life of the church and the importance of examining the nature of leadership in the parish. *The Base Church* by Charles Olsen has been around for a while, but continues to offer good insights into small-group dynamics and quality leadership in the Christian community.

I strongly recommend *Ministries: Sharing God's Gifts*, by James B. Dunning, and *How To Be a More Effective Church Leader*, by Norman Shawchuck. Finally, look at *Shared Ministry: An Integrated Approach To Leadership and Service*, by Dolore Rockers and Kenneth J. Pierre. This book is in a three-ring binder format and has some excellent practical suggestions for group dynamics and small-group ministry.

Public Worship

One resource for liturgy not previously mentioned is the collection, *Rites of the Catholic Church*. The revised rites contain a wealth of information and are useful tools for you and your community as you explore the possibilities of your public prayer life.

Another useful little book is *Preaching and the Non-Ordained*, edited by Nadine Foley, OP. It is a collection of papers given at a 1982 symposium sponsored by the Dominican Leadership Conference, and has very useful background material. Last but not least is Gabe Huck's gem, *Liturgy with Style and Grace*. This book is an easy-to-read manual on basic liturgy with content suited to novice and expert alike. Liturgy Training Publications in Chicago, which publishes this book, has a very good selection of liturgy planning aids, and I recommend them highly.

Counseling

Obviously you can't just read a book on any of these topics and become an expert. That is especially true with counseling. However, you will undoubtedly be approached by people to listen to their problems or to answer questions. Recognize your strengths or weaknesses in this area. They may simply be looking for an ear and an understanding heart. The best course may be to help find a trained counselor to help. When in doubt, listen. If you're still in doubt, refer to an expert. Make sure you know who the experts are in your community. Check with other local church leaders in the area, or the chancery. Sometimes the best advice is a good referral.

There are some good basic works you might want to review. For a good common sense approach to empathic caring, try Thomas N. Hart's *The Art of Christian Listening*. This is particularly good if you have no background in counseling. For those with some background, there is the *Clinical Handbook of Pastoral Counseling*, edited by Robert J. Wicks and others. It is a great textbook on the subject, but not one to be tackled late at night. A good introductory text is Richard P. Vaughan's *Basic Skills for Christian Counselors: An Introduction for Pastoral Ministers*.

If you feel ill-prepared in this area, check the local schools, the chancery, and your community for workshops or courses in counseling. You may have available skilled people who can serve the parish community as counselors. One method used by Father Bill Bausch in his parish in New Jersey is "one-to-one" ministry, in which people of the community volunteer to help others in the community with the same problem. A recovering alcoholic may help with other alcoholics; a parent who has lost a child may help other parents; a cancer patient may work with other victims.

Remember, don't try to do it all yourself!

Catechesis/Religious Education

If you're starting your program from scratch, check first with your diocesan office of religious education. Also check with other local parishes to see what types of programs they already offer. They can provide you good examples of materials and organizational styles which your community might then adapt. There are dozens of good religious education program materials, and we all need some help sorting through them. Take advantage of the experience of others.

We typically think of religious education programs for the children. However, we must not leave adult religious education out of the picture. Once adults feel more confident and knowledgeable, a variety of approaches can be tried with youth catechesis. In a small community with limited resources, "in-home" CCD classes can work very well. But you need a cadre of confident and competent (parent) teachers to make it work. One useful book is *Adult Education Ministry: A Parish Manual* by Richard Reichert, which gives you a good process to follow in setting up an adult education program. If you're setting up a Rite of Christian Initiation of Adults (RCIA) program, you should read *New Wine: New Wineskins* by James B. Dunning.

Another useful tool, especially for training new catechists, is *The Catechist Formation Book* by David Sork and others. For older teenagers, Kieran Sawyer, SSND, has developed several books tailored to this age group, including a textbook on confirmation, *Confirming Faith*, and *The Jesus Difference* and *The Risk of Faith*, youth ministry retreat resources.

For continuing professional education in ministry, consult your diocese and local schools. Another important resource is *Preparing Laity For Ministry*, published by the Bishops' Committee on the Laity. This catalogue lists various programs offered throughout the country on lay ministries. Some of these programs lead to advanced degrees; others provide specific ministerial training.

The document that can help put catechetical ministry in perspective is *Sharing the Light of Faith: The National Catechetical Directory for Catholics of the United States*. Published by the American bishops in 1977, it gives a wealth of information and guidance about religious education.

General Historical and Theological Information

This category is broad, and the selections I'm highlighting here are simply entry-level tools that will get you started and maybe pique your interest. I've included others in the bibliography.

Sometimes people will ask you questions about the church or some facet of church life that just need a simple answer;

for example: Where did the Rosary come from? What are the rules about fast and abstinence? A useful little reference tool for such questions and others far more profound is *The New Question Box* by John Dietzen. Perhaps you have seen Father Dietzen's syndicated column by the same name in your diocesan newspaper. The book is a compilation of his articles.

If you want one source for a good synthesis of the historical and theological development of the church, get Richard McBrien's *Catholicism*. This massive work contains a wealth of information and a great index. There are two readable histories of the church which I've found useful: *Pilgrim Church* by Father Bill Bausch and *A Concise History of the Catholic Church* by Father Thomas Bokenkotter. Bokenkotter has also written *Essential Catholicism: Dynamics of Faith and Belief*, which is a good overview of Catholic theology.

SUMMARY

I think the works cited above will give you a good starting point for reading, study, research, and reflection. There are many others listed in the bibliography.

Epilogue

Our journey has covered a lot of territory in a short time. We have considered many aspects of servant-leadership in the community of faith. My hope and prayer is that this book may serve as a support in the ministry to which God has called you and your community.

That is the real lesson. What we are about as the people of God is not our ministry at all. We are merely servants in God's ministry to humankind. It's good to reflect on that fact when we're tired, frustrated, hurt, or angry in doing ministry. We are the body of Christ in the world: "It is no longer I, but Christ living in me" (Gal 2:20).

So approach ministry as service without fear. God has called and gifted you and your community with love and peace. God will sustain you along the road. You do not journey alone.

An epilogue in a work of fiction usually sketches the future of the main characters we have come to know in the story. I hope that you have come to know yourself and your community of faith a little better after reading and using this book, but only you can write the epilogue. Your journey will be unique, just as your community is unique.

Go forth to love and serve the Lord, and each other.

Bibliography

Bausch, Rev. William J. *Pilgrim Church*. Notre Dame, IN: Fides Publishers, 1977 (revised).

———. *The Christian Parish*. Mystic, CT: Twenty-Third Publications, 1980.

———. *Ministry: Traditions, Tensions, Transitions*. Mystic, CT: Twenty-Third Publications, 1982.

———. *Take Heart, Father: A Hope-Filled Vision for Today's Priest*. Mystic, CT: Twenty-Third Publications, 1986.

Bernardin, Cardinal Joseph. *In Service of One Another: Pastoral Letter on Ministry*. Chicago: Chicago Catholic Publishing Co., 1985.

Bokenkotter, Thomas. *A Concise History of the Catholic Church*. New York: Doubleday, 1977.

———. *Essential Catholicism: Dynamics of Faith and Belief*. New York: Doubleday, 1985.

Brown, Raymond E., Joseph A. Fitzmyer, and Roland E. Murphy, eds. *The Jerome Biblical Commentary*. Englewood Cliffs, NJ: Prentice-Hall, 1968.

Brueggemann, Walter, Sharon Parks and Thomas H. Groome. *To Act Justly, Love Tenderly, Walk Humbly: An Agenda for Ministers*. New York: Paulist, 1986.

Burke, Dr. Mary P. and Rev. Eugene F. Hemrick. *Building the Local Church: Shared Responsibility in Diocesan Pastoral Councils*. Washington, DC: National Conference of Catholic Bishops, 1984.

Byers, David, ed. *The Parish in Transition: Proceedings of a Conference on the American Catholic Parish*. Washington, DC: United States Catholic Conference, 1986.

Chandler, Mary Moisson. *The Pastoral Associate and the Lay Pastor.* Collegeville, MN: The Liturgical Press, 1986.

Clinebell, Howard. *Basic Types of Pastoral Care and Counseling: Resources for the Ministry of Healing and Growth.* Nashville, TN: Abingdon Press, 1984.

Cook, Paul and Judith Zeiler. *Neighborhood Ministry Basics: A No-Nonsense Guide.* Washington, DC: Pastoral Press, 1986.

Coriden, James A., Thomas J. Green, and Donald E. Heintschel, eds. *The Code of Canon Law: A Text and Commentary.* New York: Paulist Press, 1985.

Dietzen, John J. *The New Question Box: Catholic Life in the Eighties.* Peoria, IL: Guildhall, 1985.

Doohan, Leonard. *The Lay-Centered Church: Theology & Spirituality.* Minneapolis, MN: Winston, 1984.

_____. *Laity's Mission in the Local Church: Setting a New Direction.* San Francisco: Harper & Row, 1986.

Droel, William L. and Gregory F. Augustine Pierce. *Confident and Competent: A Challenge for the Lay Church.* Chicago: ACTA Publications, 1988.

Dunning, James B. *Ministries: Sharing God's Gifts.* Winona, MN: St. Mary's Press, 1985.

_____. *New Wine: New Wineskins.* New York: Sadlier, 1981.

Dyer, George J., ed. *An American Catholic Catechism.* Chicago: Seabury Press, 1975

Edwards, O. C. *Elements of Homiletic: A Method for Preparing to Preach.* New York: Pueblo, 1982.

Fisher, Douglas, ed. *Why We Serve: Personal Stories of Catholic Lay Ministers.* Mahwah, NJ: Paulist Press, 1984.

Flannery, Austin, O.P., gen. ed. *Vatican II: The Conciliar and Post Conciliar Documents.* Northport, NY: Costello Publishing Company, 1984 (seventh printing).

Foley, Nadine, O.P., ed. *Preaching and the Non-Ordained: An Interdisciplinary Study.* Collegeville, MN: Liturgical Press, 1983.

Fowler, James W. *Stages of Faith: The Psychology of Human Development and the Quest for Meaning*. San Francisco: Harper & Row, 1981.

Fuller, Reginald H. *Preaching the Lectionary: The Word of God for the Church Today*. Collegeville, MN: Liturgical Press, 1984.

Gilmour, Peter. *The Emerging Pastor*. Kansas City, MO: Sheed & Ward, 1986.

Greeley, Andrew, Mary Durkin, John Shea, David Tracy, and William McCready. *Parish, Priest & People: New Leadership for the Local Church*. Chicago: Thomas More, 1981.

Greenleaf, Robert K. *Servant Leadership: A Journey into the Nature of Legitimate Power and Greatness*. New York: Paulist, 1977.

Hart, Thomas N. *The Art of Christian Listening*. New York: Paulist Press, 1980.

Hellwig, Monika K. *Understanding Catholicism*. Mahwah, NJ: Paulist Press, 1981

Hoge, Dean. *Future of Catholic Leadership: Responses to the Priest Shortage*. Kansas City, MO: Sheed & Ward, 1987.

Huck, Gabe. *Liturgy with Style and Grace*. Revised Edition. Chicago: Liturgy Training Publications, 1984.

Kavanagh, Aidan. *Elements of Rite: A Handbook of Liturgical Style*. New York: Pueblo, 1982.

Keating, Charles J. *The Leadership Book (revised)*. New York: Paulist Press, 1978.

Kennedy, Eugene. *The Now and Future Church: The Psychology of Being an American Catholic*. New York: Image, 1985.

_____. *Re-Imagining American Catholicism*. New York: Random House, 1985.

Komonchak, Joseph A., Mary Collins, and Dermot Lane. *The New Dictionary of Theology*. Wilmington, DE: Michael Glazier, Inc., 1987.

Kung, Hans. *The Church*. New York: Doubleday, 1967.

Lane, Dermot A. *Religious Education and the Future*. New York: Paulist, 1986.

Leckey, Dolores R. *Laity Stirring the Church: Prophetic Questions*. Philadelphia, PA: Fortress Press, 1987.

Liebard, Odile M., ed. *Clergy & Laity*. A selection of official church documents on the roles of clergy and laity, including selections from Vatican II and post-conciliar documents. Wilmington, NC: McGrath (Consortium), 1978.

McBrien, Richard P. *Catholicism*. San Francisco: Harper and Row, 1981.

_____. *Ministry: A Theological, Pastoral Handbook*. San Francisco: Harper & Row, 1987.

Miller, Robert L. and Gerard P. Weber. *Touchstone: An Activity Book for Adult Learners*. Valencia, CA: Tabor, 1987.

National Conference of Catholic Bishops. *Growing Together: Conference on Shared Ministry*. Washington, DC: National Conference of Catholic Bishops, 1980.

_____. *Called and Gifted: The American Catholic Laity*. Washington, DC: National Conference of Catholic Bishops, 1980.

_____. *To Build and Be Church: Lay Ministry Resource Packet*. Washington, DC: National Conference of Catholic Bishops, 1979.

_____. *Gifts: A Laity Reader*. Washington, DC: National Conference of Catholic Bishops, 1983.

_____. *Preparing Laity For Ministry: A Directory of Programs in the Catholic Dioceses Throughout the United States*. Washington, DC: National Conference of Catholic Bishops, 1986.

_____. *One Body: Different Gifts, Many Roles*. Washington, DC: National Conference of Catholic Bishops, 1987.

Newsome, Robert R. *The Ministering Parish: Methods and Procedures for Pastoral Organization*. New York: Paulist Press, 1982.

Notre Dame Study of Catholic Parish Life. Institute for Pastoral and Social Ministry. Notre Dame, IN: University of Notre Dame.

Olsen, Charles M. *The Base Church: Creating Community Through Multiple Forms*. Atlanta, GA: Forum, 1973.

O'Meara, Thomas Franklin. *Theology of Ministry*. New York: Paulist, 1983.

Power, David N. *Gifts That Differ: Lay Ministries Established and Unestablished*. New York: Pueblo, 1980, 1985.

Reichert, Richard. *Adult Education Ministry: A Parish Manual*. Dubuque, IA: Wm. C. Brown Company, 1987.

Ritual For Lay Presiders. Published by the Western Liturgical Conference of Canada. Regina, Saskatchewan: Liturgy Commission, 1984.

Rockers, Dolore and Kenneth J. Pierre. *Shared Ministry: An Integrated Approach to Leadership and Service*. Winona, MN: St. Mary's Press, 1984.

Sawyer, Kieran. *The Jesus Difference*. Notre Dame, IN: Ave Maria Press, 1987.

_____. *The Risk of Faith*. Notre Dame, IN: Ave Maria Press, 1988.

Schillebeeckx, Edward. *Ministry: Leadership in the Community of Jesus Christ*. New York: Crossroad, 1986.

Sharing the Light of Faith: National Catechetical Directory for Catholics of the United States. Washington, DC: United States Catholic Conference, 1979.

Shawchuck, Norman. *How To Be a More Effective Church Leader*. Irvine, CA: Spiritual Growth Resources, 1986.

Sinwell, Joseph P. and Billie Poon. *The Future of Ministry: The New England Symposium Papers*. New York: Sadlier, 1985.

Sork, David A., Don Boyd, and Maruja Sedano. *The Catechist Formation Book: Growing and Sharing*. New York: Paulist Press, 1981.

Sweetser, Thomas and Carol Wisniewski Holden. *Leadership in a Successful Parish*. San Francisco: Harper & Row, 1987.

Tavard, George H. *A Theology For Ministry*. Wilmington, DE: Michael Glazier, Inc., 1983

The Rites of the Catholic Church. English translation by The International Commission on English in the Liturgy. New York: Pueblo, 1976, 1983.

Tighe, Jeanne and Karen Szentkeresti. *Rethinking Adult Religious Education: A Practical Parish Guide*. New York: Paulist Press, 1986.

Tracy, David, ed., with Hans Kung and Johann B. Metz. *Toward Vatican III: The Work That Needs to Be Done*. New York: Seabury, 1978.

Vaughan, Richard P. *Basic Skills for Christian Counselors: An Introduction for Pastoral Ministers*. New York: Paulist, 1987.

Whitehead, Evelyn Eaton and James D. Whitehead. *Christian Life Patterns: The Psychological Challenges and Religious Invitations of Adult Life*. New York: Doubleday, 1979.

_____. *Community of Faith: Models and Strategies for Developing Christian Communities*. Minneapolis, MN: Winston-Seabury Press, 1982.

_____. *Seasons of Strength: New Visions of Adult Christian Maturing*. New York: Doubleday, 1984.

Whitehead, James D. and Evelyn Eaton Whitehead. *Method in Ministry: Theological Reflection and Christian Ministry*. Minneapolis, MN: Winston, 1980.

_____. *The Emerging Laity: Returning Leadership to the Community of Faith*. New York: Doubleday, 1986.

Wicks, Robert J., Richard D. Parsons, and Donald E. Capps, eds. *Clinical Handbook of Pastoral Counseling*. New York: Paulist Press, 1985. ·

Appendix A
Canon Law
and the Lay Pastor

Liturgical Functions

Canon 230

1. Lay men who possess the age and qualifications determined by decree of the conference of bishops can be installed on a stable basis in the ministries of lector and acolyte in accord with the prescribed liturgical rite; the conferral of these ministries, however, does not confer on these lay men a right to obtain support or remuneration from the Church.

2. Lay persons can fulfill the function of lector during liturgical actions by temporary deputation; likewise all lay persons can fulfill the functions of commentator or cantor or other functions, in accord with the norm of law.

3. When the necessity of the Church warrants it and when ministers are lacking, lay persons, even if they are not lectors or acolytes, can also supply for certain of their offices, namely, to exercise the ministry of the word, to preside over liturgical prayers, to confer baptism, and to distribute Holy Communion in accord with the prescriptions of law.

Team Ministry

Canon 517

1. When circumstances require it, the pastoral care of a parish or of several parishes together can be entrusted to a team of several priests in *solidum* with the requirement, however, that one of them should be the moderator in exercising pastoral care, that is, he should direct their combined activity and answer for it to the bishop.

2. If the diocesan bishop should decide that due to a dearth of priests a participation in the exercise of the pastoral care of a parish is to be entrusted to a deacon or to some other person who is not a priest or to a community of persons, he is to appoint some priest endowed with the powers and faculties of pastor to supervise the pastoral care.

Pastor

Canon 519

The pastor is the proper shepherd of the parish entrusted to him, exercising pastoral care in the community entrusted to him under the authority of the diocesan bishop in whose ministry of Christ he has been called to share; in accord with the norm of law he carries out for his community the duties of teaching, sanctifying and governing, with the cooperation of other presbyters or deacons and the assistance of lay members of the Christian faithful.

Canon 528

1. The pastor is obliged to see to it that the word of God in its entirety is announced to those living in the parish; for this reason he is to see to it that the lay Christian faithful are instructed in the truths of the faith, especially through the homily which is to be given on Sundays and holy days of obligation and through the catechetical formation which he is to give; he is to foster works by which the spirit of the gospel, including issues involving social justice, is promoted; he is to take special care for the Catholic education of children and of young adults; he is to make every effort with the aid of the Christian faithful, to bring the gospel message also to those who have ceased practicing their religion or who do not profess the true faith.

2. The pastor is to see to it that the Most Holy Eucharist is the center of the parish assembly of the faithful; he is to work to see to it that the Christian faithful are nourished through a devout celebration of the sacraments and especially that they frequently approach the sacrament of the Most Holy Eucharist and the sacrament of penance; he is likewise to endeavor that they are brought to the practice of family prayer as well as to a knowing and active participation in the sacred liturgy, which the pastor must supervise in his parish under the authority of the diocesan bishop, being vigilant lest any abuses creep in.

Pastoral Obligations: Governance

Canon 529

1. In order to fulfill his office in earnest the pastor should strive to come to know the faithful who have been entrusted to his care; therefore he is to visit families, sharing the cares, worries, and especially the griefs of the faithful, strengthening them in the Lord, and correcting them prudently if they are wanting in certain areas; with a

generous love he is to help the sick, particularly those close to death, refreshing them solicitously with the sacraments and commending their souls to God; he is to make a special effort to seek out the poor, the afflicted, the lonely, those exiled from their own land, and similarly those weighted down with special difficulties; he is also to labor diligently so that spouses and parents are supported in fulfilling their proper duties, and he is to foster growth in the Christian life within the family.

2. The pastor is to acknowledge and promote the proper role which the lay members of the Christian faithful have in the Church's mission by fostering their associations for religious purposes; he is to cooperate with his own bishop and with the presbyterate of the diocese in working hard so that the faithful be concerned for parochial communion and that they realize that they are members both of the diocese and of the universal Church and participate in and support efforts to promote such communion.

The Ministry of the Divine Word

Canon 759

In virtue of their baptism and confirmation lay members of the Christian faithful are witnesses to the gospel message by word and by example of a Christian life; they can also be called upon to cooperate with the bishop and presbyters in the exercise of the ministry of the word.

Canon 766

Lay persons can be admitted to preach in a church or oratory if it is necessary in certain circumstances or if it is useful in particular cases according to the prescriptions of the conference of bishops and with due regard for can. 767, #1.

Canon 767

1. Among the forms of preaching the homily is preeminent; it is a part of the liturgy itself and is reserved to a priest or to a deacon; in the homily the mysteries of faith and the norms of Christian living are to be expounded from the sacred text throughout the course of the liturgical year.

2. Whenever a congregation is present a homily is to be given at all Sunday Masses and at Masses celebrated on holy days of obligation; it cannot be omitted without a serious reason.

3. If a sufficient number of people are present it is strongly recommended that a homily also be given at Masses celebrated during the week, especially during Advent or Lent or on the occasion of some feast day or time of mourning.

4. It is the duty of the pastor or the rector of a church to see to it that these prescriptions are conscientiously observed.

Catechetical Instruction

Canon 773

There is a proper and serious duty, especially on the part of pastors of souls, to provide for the catechesis of the Christian people so that the faith of the faithful becomes living, explicit and productive through formation in doctrine and the experience of Christian living.

Canon 776

In virtue of his office the pastor is bound to provide for the catechetical formation of adults, young people and children, to which end he is to employ the services of the clerics attached to the parish, members of institutes of consecrated life and of societies of apostolic life, with due regard for the character of each institute, and lay members of the Christian faithful, above all catechists; all of these are not to refuse to furnish their services willingly unless they are legitimately impeded. The pastor is to promote and foster the role of parents in the family catechesis mentioned in can. 774, #2.

Baptism

Canon 861

1. The ordinary minister of baptism is a bishop, presbyter or deacon, with due regard for the prescription of can. 530, n. 1.

2. If the ordinary minister is absent or impeded, a catechist or other person deputed for this function by the local ordinary confers baptism licitly as does any person with the right intention in case of necessity; shepherds of souls, especially the pastor, are to be concerned that the faithful be instructed in the correct manner of baptizing.

Ministers of Viaticum

Canon 911

1. The pastor and parochial vicars, chaplains and for all who live in the house, the superior of the community in clerical religious

institutes or societies of apostolic life have the right and the duty to bring the Most Holy Eucharist to the sick in the form of Viaticum.

2. In case of necessity or with at least the presumed permission of the pastor, chaplain, or superior, who should later be notified, any priest or other minister of Holy Communion must do this.

Exposition and Benediction

Canon 943

The minister of exposition of the Most Holy Sacrament and the Eucharistic benediction is a priest or deacon; in particular circumstances the minister of exposition and reposition only, without benediction, is an acolyte, an extraordinary minister of Holy Communion or another person deputed by the local ordinary observing the prescriptions of the diocesan bishop.

Matrimony

Canon 1112

1. With the prior favorable opinion of the conference of bishops and after the permission of the Holy See has been obtained, the diocesan bishop can delegate lay persons to assist at marriages where priests or deacons are lacking.

2. A suitable lay person is to be chosen who is capable of giving instruction to those to be wed and qualified to perform the marriage liturgy correctly.

Fulfillment of Holy Day Obligation

Canon 1248

1. The precept of participating in the Mass is satisfied by assistance at a Mass which is celebrated anywhere in a Catholic rite either on the holy day or on the evening of the preceding day.

2. If because of lack of a sacred minister or for other grave cause participation in the celebration of the Eucharist is impossible, it is specially recommended that the faithful take part in the liturgy of the word if it is celebrated in the parish church or in another sacred place according to the prescriptions of the diocesan bishop, or engage in prayer for an appropriate amount of time personally or in a family or, as occasion offers, in groups of families.

Duties of Administrators

Canon 1282

All clerics or lay persons who through a legitimate title take part in administration of ecclesiastical goods are bound to fulfill their duties in the name of the Church and in accord with the norm of law.

Administrators Not Designated As Such

Canon 1289

Even if they are not bound to administration by the title of an ecclesiastical office, administrators cannot relinquish their responsibilities on their own initiative; if, however, the Church is harmed by such an arbitrary abandonment of duty they are bound to restitution.

Appendix B
Sample Parish Council Guidelines

MODEL BY-LAWS FOR PARISH COUNCILS

ARTICLE I — NAME

The name of this body shall be (   ) Parish Council, hereinafter referred to as "the Council".

ARTICLE II — PURPOSES

Section 1. The purposes of the Parish Council shall be:

a) Priorities & Planning — To determine priorities and plan with vision for the future.

b) Implementation — To ensure that programs and activities of the parish are carried out by Commissions.

c) Involvement — To involve everyone in the work of the parish.

d) Shared Decision-Making — To enable as many people as possible to contribute to the process of decision-making in the parish.

e) Cooperation with Diocese — To cooperate with diocesan departments and through the Deanery Council with other parishes and to carry out its work according to the priorities of the Diocese and under its guidance.

f) Contribution to Diocese — To contribute to the formulation of diocesan goals and programs.

ARTICLE III — MEMBERSHIP

Section 1. Categories

a) Any registered member of the parish, eighteen years of age or older, is eligible to be a member of the Council. This minimum age limit need not apply to youth representatives chosen according to local custom.

b) The following are ex-officio members of the Council: the pastor, associate pastors, pastoral associates, and the six Commission chairpersons; also a representative of religious working for the parish, deacons, directors of religious education, director of worship, youth ministers, and the school principal, if these persons are providing professional service for the parish. All ex-officio members of the Council, except for the pastor, have full voting privileges.

c) At least twelve, nor more than fifteen, members of the Council shall be elected by the parish, one-third of these being elected each year.

d) Up to two persons may be appointed by the Pastor to the Council, in order to ensure a balanced representation from all groups in the parish, especially youth.

Section 2. Tenure

a) The term of office for elected or appointed members shall last for three years.

b) No elected or appointed member shall serve more than two consecutive terms, after which the member will be ineligible for one year. An appointment to fill a vacancy shall be counted as a term.

c) Any elected or appointed member absent for three regular meetings without having notified the president in advance of the meeting shall lose his or her membership on the Council.

Section 3. To fill a vacancy on the Council the existing members shall select and appoint a qualified person to complete the unexpired term.

ARTICLE IV — ELECTIONS

Section 1. Election Committee

a) At the regular meeting held in March, the Council shall appoint three or five persons with their previous consent, to serve as an Election Committee.

b) The duties of this committee are:

   1) to prepare a slate of candidates to be voted upon by the entire parish through one of the following processes:

      a) by conducting a primary election

      b) by serving as a Nominating Committee

   2) to inform them of what the Council is and how it operates before obtaining their consent to run as candidates

   3) to conduct the election according to Council policy.

Section 2. Voting

a) Voting will take place by secret ballot at a time during April or May to be determined by the Council.

b) Any registered member of the parish eighteen years of age or older shall be entitled to vote.

c) The ideal number of candidates shall be at least twice the number of vacancies, although for serious reasons the candidates could be less numerous provided they exceed the number of vacancies.

d) Provision will be made on the ballot for write-in candidates.

ARTICLE V — THE PASTOR ON THE COUNCIL

(The roles listed below apply only to the Pastor's relationship to the Parish Council. They do not attempt to describe his many other responsibilities toward the parish.)

Section 1. As one of the People of God, the Pastor joins with the other members to make the Council a special family of persons bound together in friendship and support, personal sharing and mutual respect.

Section 2. As the spiritual guide of the parish, the Pastor calls for the work of the Council to grow from the action of the Holy Spirit. Through common prayer with the other members and a tone of gentle presence to the Spirit, he helps the Council see all their work as a spiritual service.

Section 3. As the leader of the parish, the Pastor brings a sense of vision and direction to the Council. He calls for professionalism in the planning and conduct of programs, affirms the gifts parishioners have received for the common good of the Church, and by his enthusiasm and care motivates people to be involved and responsible.

Section 4. Other members of the Pastoral Staff, according to their responsibilities in the parish, should share in this role of the Pastor.

ARTICLE VI — OFFICERS

Section 1. The officers of the Council shall be a President, Vice-President, and Secretary.

Section 2. The members of the incoming Council shall, at their first meeting after the election, vote among themselves for the three officers specified in Section 1 above. After nominations, voting shall be by secret ballot. The majority vote of members present shall determine the winners. Each office shall be taken individually, to permit candidates not elected to be nominated for another office.

Section 3. The duties of the President focus upon the effective operation of the Council (while the Pastor's role focuses upon the whole parish). The duties of the President are:

a) to preside at all meetings

b) to work closely with the pastor in discharging the following responsibilities:

    1) to call special meetings

    2) to appoint, after consulting the Council, the chairpersons of Parish Council Commissions and the members of special committees

      3) to develop the agenda for all Council meetings

  c) to monitor the progress of programs being carried out through the Commissions

  d) to ensure that each Council member, except the officers, is serving on a Commission.

Section 4. The duties of the Vice-President are:

  a) to assume the duties of the President in his absence or at his request

  b) to work with the President in monitoring the work of the Commissions.

Section 5. The duties of the Secretary are:

  a) to keep accurate minutes of the Council meetings

  b) a week prior to the next Council meeting, to mail the following materials to the members:

      1) minutes of the last Council meeting

      2) agenda for the next meeting

      3) any pertinent background information

  c) to be responsible for all correspondence of the Council.

Section 6. Vacancies

  a) If a vacancy occurs in the office of president, the vice-president will assume the office and serve the remainder of the term.

  b) If a vacancy occurs in the office of the vice-president or the secretary, a successor should be elected from among the Council members to serve the unexpired portion of the term.

ARTICLE VII — COMMISSIONS

Section 1. The Standing Commissions of the Parish Council shall be: Church Life, Worship and Spirituality, Religious Education, Social Justice and Peace, Family Life, and Finance and Administration. They should always strive to work with persons who have professional competence in the areas being addressed by a Commission.

Section 2. The responsibilities of the Church Life Commission are:

Section 3. The responsibilities of the Worship and Spirituality Commission are:

Section 4. The responsibilities of the Religious Education Commission are:

Section 5. The responsibilities of the Social Justice and Peace Commission are:

Section 6. The responsibilities of the Family Life Commission are:

Section 7. The responsibilities of the Finance and Administration Commission are:

Section 8. Each member of the Council except the officers shall serve on one of the Commissions, but not on more than one.

Section 9. The chairpersons of the Commissions should be chosen for their competence and leadership abilities. It is not necessary that they be chosen from the Council membership; they may be taken from the parish at large. All chairpersons, even those chosen from outside the Council, shall have full voting rights. The President should choose the chairpersons. He should work closely with the Pastor in making these selections, and he may also consult the Parish Council.

Section 10. The chairpersons of each Commission shall be free to recruit for his or her Commission parishioners who are not members of the Council. These parishioners should make up the great majority of each Commission.

Section 11. Each Commission should meet at least once between the meetings of the Council.

Section 12. All Commissions and committees are accountable to the Council and may only implement programs which have been previously approved by the Council either in the Pastoral Plan or through subsequent action.

Section 13. For the sake of accuracy, and to assist the Council Secretary, written reports of the Commission meetings should be prepared for the Council.

ARTICLE VIII — COUNCIL MEETINGS

Section 1. All meetings of the Council shall be open to the parish. Meetings shall be publicized in advance.

Section 2. Regular meetings of the Council shall be held monthly on such days as may be determined by the Council.

Section 3. With the agreement of the Pastor, special meetings may be called by the President or any four members of the Council acting jointly.

Section 4. More than half of the full membership of the Council must be present for the Council to have a meeting.

Section 5. The order of procedure at Council meetings shall be a matter of Council policy.

Section 6. Although the Council may pass motions by majority vote, if necessary, the Council should strive to make its decisions through consensus (a decision which all the Council members can at least live with, even the few who do not endorse it fully).

Section 7. As the Council conducts its business, the Pastor expresses his opinion on the items preferably toward the end of the discussion. He does not, however, vote on the motion.

Section 8. All decisions of the Council become authoritative or final only with the assent of the Pastor. This responsibility of the Pastor will usually be carried out informally in the course of the discussion.

ARTICLE IX — DUE PROCESS PROCEDURE

In a dispute between the Parish Council and the Pastor, a sincere attempt at resolution through dialogue and prayer must first be attempted within the parish. If the dispute cannot be resolved to the satisfaction of the parties involved, it may be appealed: first to the Dean as mediator if both parties are consenting, and then, if necessary, to the Diocesan Board of Conciliation and Arbitration.

ARTICLE X — AMENDMENT

These by-laws may be amended at any regular meeting of the Council by a two-thirds vote, provided that the proposal to amend was submitted in writing at the previous regular Council meeting.

PURPOSES

OF THE CHURCH IN THE DIOCESE OF PORTLAND

INTRODUCTION

The Catholic Church that we make up as a people is not created simply by our efforts. It is called into existence by the Father speaking through his Son and is built up by our graced cooperation with the Holy Spirit. The initiative for everything we do as a holy people comes from his Spirit; and so it is imperative that we constantly examine our efforts, to insure that their origin is from Him.

The purposes of the Church express seven different dimensions of what it means for us to be the Catholic Church. These dimensions include worship, proclamation of the gospel, community, ecumenism, social justice, mutual responsibility and service. Everything we do must grow from these purposes; and for that reason the process of Pastoral Planning begins with a study of them and refers back to them at every step.

PURPOSES

1. To praise and glorify God the Father through Jesus His Son in the Holy Spirit.

2. To proclaim the Good News of Salvation in Christ Jesus and thus give full meaning to human life.

3. To form Christian communities alive with the Holy Spirit.

4. To advance unity among Christians and to increase the awareness of the presence of God within the Church and beyond the Church.

5. To promote social justice by fostering the fullest development of every person.

6. To develop in all persons the awareness that they are responsible the one for the other.

7. To express the compassion of Christ by acts of service to those in need.

AREAS OF CONCERN

1. Church Life
2. Worship and Spirituality
3. Education
4. Social Justice and Peace
5. Family Life
6. Finance and Administration

RESPONSIBILITIES WITHIN THE PARISH

PASTORAL STAFF

LEADERSHIP

To lead the ministry of the entire parish, the action that is carried out by all members under the inspiration of the Holy Spirit.

PROCLAMATION

To proclaim the Word of God in the power of the Spirit, that increases the understanding and commitment of the faithful and draws others into their midst.

WORSHIP

To have exemplary lives of prayer and to guide the parish in the worship of the Father and in the development of their spiritual lives.

COMMUNITY

To join together around themselves, the members of the parish as a family who know and love one another.

SERVICE

To be models of compassionate service and the pursuit of justice.

PARISH COUNCIL
(With the Direction of the Pastor)

PRIORITIES
& PLANNING

To determine parish priorities and plan with vision for the future.

COORDINATION

To coordinate the current programs and activities of the parish.

INVOLVEMENT

To involve everyone in the work of the parish.

SHARED DECISION-
MAKING

To enable as many people as possible to contribute to the process of decision-making in the parish.

COOPERATION
WITH DIOCESE

To cooperate with diocesan departments and through the Deanery Council with other parishes and to carry out its ministry according to the priorities of the Diocese and under its guidance.

CONTRIBUTION
TO DIOCESE

To contribute to the formulation of diocesan goals and programs.

CHURCH LIFE COMMISSION

COMMUNITY
SPIRIT

To assist in making the parish a community
in which persons can come to know one another, to share their lives and concerns, and to
find support for their faith.

COMMUNICATION

To ensure good communications among all
groups in the parish and to provide effective
publicity for parish events.

ECUMENISM

To initiate and support the growth of mutual
understanding and common action among the
different Christian Churches.

EVANGELIZATION

To maintain active programs of reaching out to
non-practicing Catholics and the unchurched.

WORSHIP & SPIRITUALITY COMMISSION

SACRAMENTAL
PRAYER

To plan the celebration of the sacraments,
especially the Holy Eucharist, with great care, so
that they are occasions for communal prayer that
nourish and uplift the assembly.

TEACHING
PRAYER

To teach people how to pray, including the
nature of prayer and the steps in its growth.

PRAYER THROUGH
THE DAY

To teach people to pray the Liturgy of the
Hours with understanding and devotion.

RETREATS

To nourish the faith of parishioners in retreats,
days of recollection, devotions and other programs of spiritual enrichment.

EDUCATION COMMISSION

TEACHING THE
FAITH

To develop for every age group in the parish
a religious education program of high quality,
that transmits the teachings and customs of the
Church.

TEACHING THE
BIBLE

To teach everyone to read the Bible with
understanding and fidelity.

PREPARATION FOR THE SACRAMENTS
To have good programs of catechesis for individuals and their families who are about to celebrate the sacraments.

CATHOLIC SCHOOLS
Where Catholic schools exist, to insure that they offer an environment that calls forth the desire for God, through prayer and appropriate theological reflections, and the desire to learn, through the excellence and variety of teachers and programs.

SOCIAL JUSTICE AND PEACE COMMISSION

EDUCATION ABOUT JUSTICE
To educate the parish in the teachings of the Church on social justice and in the ways that work for social justice forms an essential part of being a Christian.

EDUCATION ABOUT PARTICULAR ISSUES
To educate the people about particular problems of social justice and peace in their parish and about other social issues of wider concern.

LOCAL OUTREACH
To investigate and coordinate the parish response to problems of social justice within the area of the parish, especially to the needs of the poor, the sick, the oppressed and the imprisoned.

FAMILY LIFE COMMISSION

MARITAL PREPARATION
To provide for those about to enter marriage, prolonged and substantive training in the dynamics of marital life and in the theology of marriage.

FAMILY ENRICHMENT
To offer a variety of programs that support and encourage the growth of family life, especially in the areas of communications, the sharing of self, and the spirituality of the family.

YOUTH
To provide counsel and support for youth, especially concerning their self image, relations with peers and family relationships.

FINANCE & ADMINISTRATION COMMISSION

CENSUS
To maintain an accurate census of membership.

FINANCIAL EDUCATION
To educate the parish about financial priorities and needs.

FUND RAISING

To stimulate greater financial responsibility by the members of the parish.

BUDGET
PREPARATION

To prepare through consultation with all commissions an annual budget for the coming year.

DISBURSEMENT
SUPERVISION

To oversee the disbursement of funds according to the current budget.

GENERAL
FINANCIAL
SUPERVISION

To oversee all construction and repairs, parish insurance coverage, the preparation of quarterly and annual financial reports and the Catholic Charities Appeal.

PLANT INVENTORY
& REPLACEMENT

To maintain an inventory and assessment of all parish equipment, furnishings and buildings; and to prepare a schedule for their replacement or renewal.

COLLECTING DATA ON THE PARISH

Possible Data

1. Demographic:

   - parish population: number of families, number of individuals
   - parish population forecasts — growth, decline
   - age distribution of parish
   - geographic distribution of parish residents
   - school age total Catholic population: elementary, high
   - numbers attending religion classes: elementary, high
   - numbers attending private schools: elementary, high
   - numbers attending public schools: elementary, high

2. Sacramental:

   - Sacramental statistics
   - Baptism, number for each of the previous 3 years
   - Weddings for each of the previous 3 years
   - Shut-ins
   - Number of Deaths in parish over the last 3 years

3. Attitudinal:

   To discover what people think about the parish (strengths, weaknesses) N.B. (Be sure to consult ALL elements of the parish and not to limit yourself to the regular church-going Catholic.)

   - Written questionnaire filled out at Mass
   - Interviews
   - Open forums — for example, to determine needs of inactive Catholics.

4. Economic:

   - Parish financial statement for past 3 years
   - Average Sunday collection

- Average parishioner offering
- School financial statement for past 3 years
- Total parish budget — current & projected for following year
- Amount spent on religious education of children:
  a) Religious Education Program: total cost, cost per pupil
  b) Parish School: total cost, cost per pupil

Sources of Information for Parish Data

- Parish census
- Sacramental records
- Parish School & Religious Education Program Records
- Parish & School financial statements

BASIC RESEARCH

NEW TRENDS THAT WILL AFFECT THE LIFE OF OUR PARISH
• RELIGION • POPULATION • ECONOMY •
• PERSONNEL • NEIGHBORHOOD • ETC. •

MAJOR
ONGOING PROGRAMS
CHURCH LIFE COMMISSION

1.

2.

3.

4.

5.

6.

WORSHIP & SPIRITUALITY COMMISSION

1.

2.

3.

4.

5.
6.

EDUCATION COMMISSION

1.

2.

3.

4.

5.

6.

SOCIAL JUSTICE AND PEACE COMMISSION

1.

2.

3.

4.

5.

6.

FAMILY LIFE COMMISSION

1.

2.

3.

4.

5.

6.

FINANCE & ADMINISTRATION COMMISSION

1.

2.

3.

4.

5.

6.

CHARACTERISTICS OF A GOOD GOAL

It must:

1. **Begin with an infinitive verb:** Use verbs that clearly express action — e.g., "to enlist, to train, and to schedule."

2. **Contain only one central event:** If you have two steps forward, then write two Goals. A Goal should be clear and short — two or three typewritten lines.

3. **Have a terminal point** that can be attained.
   Example of a bad Goal: To reach out to the poor within our community.
   Example of a good Goal: To plan, staff and operate a thrift shop that will serve a minimum of one poor family a week.

4. **Be concrete and specific:** No generalities. State exactly what change you intend to bring about. Be concrete and practical. A bad Goal would be: "To work with youth of the parish".

5. **Be measurable:** At the end of the 5 years, we should be able to determine whether the Goal has been attained or not and to what degree (%). Use numbers or percentages of concrete achievements that will be evident in 5 years — e.g., "to increase attendance at adult religion courses by 30%".

6. **Provide a step forward:** A goal that maintains the "status quo" is not a Goal. Such a bad Goal could read: "To continue our confirmation program for the youth of the parish".

7. **Be challenging enough to require 5 years to attain.** "To hold a commissioning service for Parish Council members" is not a Goal; it does not require 5 years to reach.

8. **Be capable of being subdivided into one-year Objectives:** "To hold one dance" is not a Goal because it does not require five years to implement. This dance, if it will require a good part of the year to plan and to carry out, can be considered as an Objective. This Objective would be placed under a broader Goal, such as: "To develop parish spirit by actively involving 50 new families in parish activities".

9. **Be within control of the parish:** You cannot set for yourself a Goal over which you have no control or for which you do not have the resources. For example, a parish could not set as its Goal: "To maintain an active liturgical committee in every parish of the diocese".

HOW TO DEVELOP A GOOD OBJECTIVE

It must:

1. **Begin with an infinitive verb:** Use verbs that clearly express action — e.g. — to enlist, train, to schedule, etc.

2. **Contain only one central event:** If you have two central thoughts, then write two Objectives. An Objective should be clear and short — two or three typewritten lines.

3. **Have a terminal point** that can be attained.
   Example of a bad Objective: "To have more religion teachers".
   Example of a good Objective: "To recruit and train 10 religion teachers".

4. **Be concrete and specific:** No generalities. State exactly what change you intend to bring about. Remember to state HOW you intend to do it not WHAT you intend to do. The WHAT was taken care of in the Goal. For example, a Goal says WHAT: "To involve 50% of the parents in the religious education of their children". An Objective says HOW: "To hold three special programs for the parents of children receiving Baptism, First Communion and First Penance".

5. **Be measurable:** At the end of the year, we should be able to determine whether the objective has been attained or not and to what degree (%). Use numbers (e.g., to recruit and train 10 Eucharistic Ministers) or percentages (e.g., to increase our Social Justice Commission by 50%) that can be evaluated at the end of the year.

6. **Provide a step forward:** an Objective that maintains the status quo is not an Objective. Bad Objective: "To continue our Religion Class".

7. **Be challenging enough** to require effort for the greater part of a year: "To hold an open house at the school" is not a good Objective because it does not require a year to implement. It should be included, rather, as a step in the time schedule under a larger program. The Objective could be: "To hold 3 programs that will increase the awareness of parishioners towards our school".

8. **Be within the control of the parish:** You can only set Objectives over which you have control and for which you have the resources.

You *cannot*, for example, set as an Objective: "To organize a Training Program for Lectors in the Deanery". That would be an Objective for the Deanery to set, not the parish.

COMMISSION:

GOAL NO:

OBJECTIVE NO.	
PERSON RESPONSIBLE:	
TIMETABLE OF STEPS:	
SELF-EVALUATION:	DIFFICULTIES ENCOUNTERED

OBJECTIVE NO.	
PERSON RESPONSIBLE:	
TIMETABLE OF STEPS:	
SELF-EVALUATION:	DIFFICULTIES ENCOUNTERED

OUR COVENANT

This Pastoral Plan is a statement of the major steps forward which we have agreed to take, as a Christian community, during the coming year — July 1 to June 30.

Listed below are the main elements of the mutual commitment of the parish and of the Diocese.

PARISH

1. In the preparation of this Pastoral Plan, we have attempted to keep in mind:

   a. The reasons for the Church's presence.

   b. The needs of the religious and secular community.

2. We submit this Plan as a sign of our close union with the Diocese and as an instrument of communication with our Bishop.

3. We commit ourselves to implement the programs stated herein and to conduct an annual evaluation of our performance.

DIOCESE

1. I intend to give serious consideration to the goals presented in this Pastoral Plan in the designing of diocesan programs.

2. Personally and through the efforts of the diocesan departments, I propose to offer support and leadership in realizing this Plan.

3. In order to ensure good communications within the Diocese, I will share the programs submitted in this Plan with all the parishes and the departments.

For the Parish of: _____

Pastor: _____

Parish Council
President:_____

Date· _____

For the Diocese of Portland

Bishop of
Portland:_____

Evaluating the Pastoral Plan

I. Quarterly Review

A. Review the objectives of each Commission

- Are the objectives being accomplished? If so, how many and at what rate of completion?

- What difficulties are being encountered?

- Do changes need to be made, or are the objectives still valid?

B. Review the goals of each Commission

- Are additional resources required?

- Should goals be considered for future modifications or elimination for next year?

- Should additional goals be developed for next year's plan?

II. Annual Review

This process is similar to the Quarterly Review, except that the data for the entire year is examined. This will be much easier if the quarterly review is done as accurately and as detailed as possible.

III. Deanery Review

Following completion, the Annual Review is submitted to a review by a Deanery Review Team. This process will include an assessment of the content of the Goals and Objectives of the pastoral plan and their implementation. It will also review the technical correctness of the planning process.